A Guid

Motor Barge Handling

Edward Burrell

04417

Published by Edward Burrell
The Boathouse
27 Lower Hampton Road
Sunbury on Thames
TW16 5PR

edward.burrell@ntlworld.com

Graphics and illustrations designed by the author and
executed by Cristiane Watanabe.

All photos by Pamela and Edward Burrell except where
otherwise credited.

Cover photo: 'Angelus' at Sunbury Lock on the Thames.

Prepared by Back-In-Print Books Ltd, London
www.backinprint.co.uk
Printed and bound in Great Britain by
Antony Rowe Ltd, Eastbourne.

*This book is dedicated to all the
bridges, moorings, bollards, tunnels and locks
which took a knock
for the want of training of barge skippers.*

Barges entering West India Dock, Canary Wharf for DBA rally

ACKNOWLEDGEMENTS

I would like to thank all those from whom I've learned my skills. Especially all those who have been so gracious when I have 'bumped' into them.

In the preparation of this book I'd like to thank the many people who have contributed their knowledge, experience and input.

Stefan Fritz	'de Jelte'	28m	sailing Klipper
Capt. John Bowen	'Rietvink'	16m	Beurtship
John Tims	'Atlas'	21m	Dutch Tug
Tony Woodward	'Daybreak'	19m	Humber Keel
Sir Adrian Stott bt.	'Onx'	21m	Katwijker
Capt. Ian Ferguson	'Alieda'	24m	Stevenaak
Chris Ries	'Mooi Aak'	21m	Luxemotor
and			
Marlow Ropes			

Disclaimers

All barges are different and the circumstances in which they are being used will vary. The author cannot accept any responsibility howsoever caused for any actions or consequences which may occur as a result of reading this book, acting upon its contents or thinking you know what you are doing

About the Author.

My life on the river started in 1974. I bought a rotten old 72ft motor gunboat on the Thames under Twickenham Railway Bridge. Against all the odds I managed to keep it afloat for a few years, sold it for a small profit, and bought a little 35ft wooden boat. The hull was sound and I built a new superstructure. It was home to me and my two children until I sold it for a rather better profit. This gave me half of the price of my first Dutch barge. 'Hoop op Zegen' is a small Tjalk built in 1898 and just under 15m. The ship needed quite a lot of work. In the end I gutted it and rebuilt the whole thing. With a new engine I was ready to go barging. Local friends, who already had small barges, showed me how to handle it.

My training ground was ideal. Situated just upstream of Richmond half-tide sluices, most of the time the water level was constant and easily managed. When the tide came in,, the river filled all the way to Teddington. You could take a falling tide down to London, stay over until the tide turned, and ride it back to Richmond again. I also managed a few trips down to the Medway. It was on one of these, when a sudden fog descended, that I decided I should go to school and get my Day Skipper's ticket. Subsequently this was followed by the ICC – International Certificate of Competence.

In 1989, re-married and with a young daughter, we spotted a residential mooring for sale in Sunbury on Thames. We put in a bid and bought it. With a bigger mooring at our disposal and a growing daughter we decided to go for a larger barge. 'Angelus' came to our notice lying on the Grand Union Canal near Hemel Hempstead. She was 19.8m, the perfect size, and offered an extra cabin aft of the wheelhouse. Our 'new' barge, built in 1884, was even older than 'Hoop'. Unfortunately the conversion which had been done when she was brought over to the UK was not suitable. Once more, I decided to gut the ship and start again. At least this way you know every rivet, wire and pipe intimately. There is no such thing as a perfect barge but we can live with the compromises we have achieved. Cruising was suspended for a couple of years but as soon as we could we were on the move again. As well as cruising the Thames we try and get down to the sea each year. Regular visitors to the Swale Smack & Barge match, we travel the East Coast between North Kent and Suffolk. In 2002 we crossed the channel for the DBA 10th Party in Ghent. From there we cruised north through the Netherlands before returning home.

From 1997 to 2002 I was Chairman of DBA The Barge Association, editor of their magazine 'Blue Flag', winning IWA awards twice for best amateur club magazine, and a contributor to DBA's 'The Barge Buyer's Handbook'.

Strictly Come Barging!

Angelus

was built in 1884 in Dordrecht, in the Netherlands.

She is an example of a rare Dutch barge known as a Kraak (pron: crark) There are only about 35 of these ships surviving in Holland today. Built of riveted iron she carried a much larger mast and was sailed or towed.

When diesel engines were introduced, the rudder was moved aft to accommodate the propeller. It is thought she was built to carry stone and continued in trade as a refueling ship in Brussels until 1981.

In rebuilding the coachroof we sought to retain the original sweep of the elegant hull. She was fitted with a new mast and steadying sail rig, and the boom also acts as a derrick for lifting heavy items including the dinghy. She makes regular trips to the Medway, North Kent, and the East Coast. In 2002 she completed a two month trip through Belgium and the Netherlands returning the 'spirit' who inhabited the fo'castle to his home port. Only experienced by our daughter, he was young and benign. When we returned she came aboard, went into her cabin and declared, "He's gone, you know."

Angelus off the Belgian coast en route cross-Channel to Ghent.
Photo by Malcom Pumphrey

INTRODUCTION

This *Guide to Motor Barge Handling* looks at the whys and the wherefores of motor barges. In this context we are talking about vessels which were originally designed and built for inland commercial shipping. In general these will be of Dutch origin built of iron or steel and have been adapted for private pleasure and residential use. However there is a growing market for newly built replica ships to which this guide also applies. Suggestions are offered on how to handle your barge based on some of the basic elements of these vessels and how such elements affect their movement.

The book sets out, through easy text and illustrations, to introduce you to the specifics of handling motor barges of a particular size. Typically these ships will be between 15m and 35m in length with a beam in excess of 3m, a draught of 1m plus and built of iron or steel. There are many books and courses relating to various aspects of seamanship and navigation and to general aspects of boating - some of which apply to barging. This book does not attempt to replicate any of these. The assumption has been made that the reader has a basic experience of boating of some kind since handling barges of this size is a serious responsibility.

Written for the less experienced skippers and crew alike it is designed to bring some knowledge, understanding, confidence and thereby pleasure and safety to their barging. More experienced bargees may like to share the book with their crews For the purpose of comprehension the use of nautical terms is limited but a glossary includes those relevant to barges.

After more than 25 years of owning, converting, cruising and living on my own barges I am conscious of the fact that there is still more to learn and in the process of writing this book my own knowledge has certainly increased. There will never be a definitive guide and there is no substitute for the real thing. The more hands-on experience and practice you can get, the better. Meanwhile I hope this helps you on your way.

Edward Burrell   Spring 2005

CONTENTS

Key to Illustrations

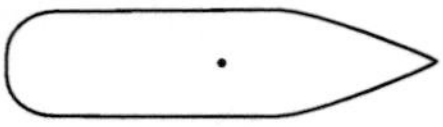

pivot point

going forward

going astern

engine gear direction

direction prop will walk

direction of ship movement

direction of prop thrust

direction of major current

direction of minor current

wind

drift vector

PREFACE

The book sets out to introduce some of the basic principles of barge handling. It looks at barges, the hull and equipment and the physics involved in the movement of this heavy lump of metal through the water.

The book is divided into five parts. Part 1 looks at the basic elements of the barge itself and the component parts which affect its movement. Part 2 looks at techniques for handling the barge and how to make it behave the way you want. Part 3 is dedicated to the subject of ropes and warps. Part 4 looks at some of the associated equipment and aspects of the barge. The final part covers subjects related to the management of a barge.

You don't actually 'drive' a barge.
It is not on rails, it is adrift.

Handling a barge is all about using and balancing the forces available to you.

The Primary Rule – Do It Slowly

The rule is – do it slowly – or even more slowly. This was the first thing that was drummed into me and it is the most valuable lesson. It is quite easy to get a barge to move but stopping it is quite another matter. Most barges will drift on for several hundred metres when taken out of gear.

Generally speaking it is easier to manage a barge than a yacht or cruiser. A barge has straight sides, decks to walk along and space on the bow and stern to make 'working' the ship much more comfortable. In spite of its size and weight you are doing everything slowly which gives time to move about and be organised.

Most of the manoeuvres and techniques described in this book are standard practice for barge handling. In a few cases more advanced techniques are discussed. It is recommended that these are not attempted until a full command and experience of the basics has been achieved. They are indicated as **Advanced Technique**.

Naturally the book reflects my own experience and there will be other techniques and styles which are equally valid. You, your crew and your barge will develop your own.

Part One

BASIC ELEMENTS

Part One covers those elements of a barge and its construction which are relevant to its management through the water. Other aspects concerning equipment and parts are covered in more detail in Part Four.

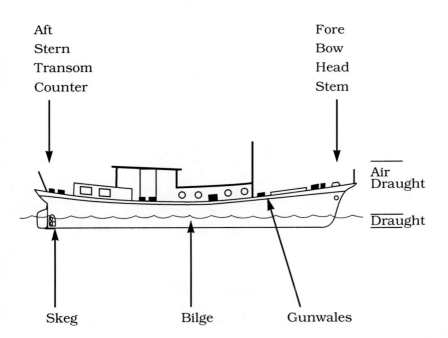

Aft
Stern
Transom
Counter

Fore
Bow
Head
Stem

Air Draught

Draught

Skeg   Bilge   Gunwales

HULL & DYNAMICS

Pivot Point

A vessel has a pivot point somewhere along the length around which the hull will rotate. The exact position depends on the hull shape and weight distribution. For example, a sailing boat with a long deep keel and most of its weight nearer the aft end will have a pivot point nearer the stern. Barges tend to pivot somewhere between a third and two thirds from the bow. Knowing where your pivot point is will dictate many of your manoeuvres and bring precision to your barge handling. You can easily find this position on a barge by standing on the wharf beside it and, on slack lines, pushing it out with your foot. The pivot point is where, when pushed, the barge moves out parallel to the bank.

However this point moves depending on the circumstances and, when going astern for example, it moves nearer the aft end.

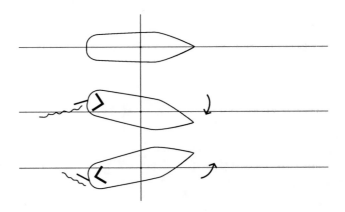

Drift & Grip

Motor barges, generally speaking, come with flat bottoms and round bilges. This allows them to navigate in shallow waters as well as take to the ground in an upright position. However this means that there is nothing inherent in the shape to prevent it from drifting, slipping and sliding sideways. Round bilges on old barges will slip more than square ones (hard chined replica barges) which offer a small degree of resistance.

Bow & Stern

Hull shapes vary enormously. Whether you have a Tjalk, Klipper, Aak or Luxemotor doesn't affect the principles of how the barge moves. Luxemotors, for example, have a sharper bow shape to cut through the water and have a finer stern. Tjalken and Aaken are more rounded and take a bluffer approach at both ends. Remember, older ships were designed for sailing without propellers (which were added later). However some of the recently built replica barges often have a very blunt stern. This reduces the hydro-dynamic flow to the propeller and rudder and will make the ship harder to handle. Generally the bluffer barges handle less well than those designed as motor barges.

Windage

All the parts of your ship which are above the water line are subject to one of the key forces at work. Wind. Think of the sides of your barge as a sail. A barge of 20m with coachroof, wheelhouse and aft cabin like mine has a 'sail' area of about 35sq m. This is a big sail. A larger barge with a high-sided coachroof presents an even bigger area. Beam on to the wind you will be carried along by this alone. If you have the wind on your bow or astern the effects will be minimal on handling. But sticking your nose out of a sheltered dock entrance or canal into a side wind can have dramatic effects on your course. *See* **Flags and Wind Indicators**.

Draught

The draught of barges is generally between 0.8m and 1.5 m. Usually they will be ballasted to be shallower at the fore and deeper at the stern. Often the bottom rudder mountings will produce a deeper skeg profile. Barges which don't have sufficient ballast will be more prone to skidding across the surface. A well-ballasted and trimmed ship handles better by being balanced in the water. The draught at the bow should be no less than 60% and ideally nearer 90% of the stern draught. If the bow is too shallow your turning point will be moved aft and the ship will be harder to steer. In some rare cases you may find that the barge has a shallow keel running down the centre line. This may be a small help in reducing sideslip but is a disadvantage when taking to the ground. You won't sit down flat. Care should be taken when crossing shallow sills or dry docking the barge if anything is protuding lower than the flat area of the bottom.

Hull Dynamics

Not only does a barge have a centre point on which it pivots, it also has a centre of gravity. A fully laden cargo barge will have a low centre as it settles down into the water. A converted barge which carries a lot of steelwork in the cabin conversion above deck level and minimal ballast raises its centre of gravity. Combined with a flat bottom and round bilges this creates a shape which will roll, pitch and yaw. The lower the centre of gravity the better the barge will perform especially at sea.

Weight

A barge which is 20m x 4.2m x 1m weighs about 50 tonnes. Here is a rough formula for calculating this. Add the draught in metres at the bow and at the stern, multiply by 0.5, multiply by length (waterline) and by beam (midship). Finally multiply by a factor which has been estimated at about 0.8 which compensates for the fact that a ship is not a box. The result is, roughly, your displacement weight in tonnes. Heavier barges will carry more drift or sideslip through the water which needs to be taken into account.

PROPELLER

Propellers have either a Left Hand (anti-clockwise) or Right Hand (clockwise) pitch depending on rotation when going ahead and viewed from astern. They typically have either 3 or 4 blades. The size and efficiency will affect your barge's movement.

Paddle Wheel Effect

The correct name is Transverse Thrust but it is known as 'Prop Walk'. It is also referred to as 'Kick' meaning the direction in which the stern 'kicks' when reversing. As the propeller turns, the fact that the blades are angled (pitched) means that they are not only trying to move the barge forward through the water, they are also trying to paddle it round sideways. The direction in which this occurs depends on the direction of propeller rotation. It has the tendency, when going forwards, to steer the barge slightly off to one side. You will find yourself compensating for this without realising it.

However, when going astern, the effect is much more marked and the 'paddle wheel' effect will walk the barge sideways quite noticeably. This is because vessels are designed to work best when going forward. The flow of water past the hull and the thrust from propeller onto rudder combine to give you steerage. When going astern everything is going in the wrong direction. It happens for a number of reasons. The propeller paddling round, the pitch of the prop blades pushing the water away at an angle, the lower blade being in deeper water and the shape of your stern all conspire to move the barge sideways.

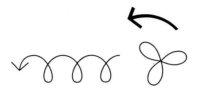

Prop walk can become more pronounced the longer and harder you go astern. If you only use very short bursts then it won't develop the walk as much. However it can be cancelled out or even reversed by strong side winds.

How to use this effect is referred to in Part Two.

RUDDERS

The purpose of the rudder is to deflect the flow of water at the stern thereby sending the vessel in a different direction. There are a lot of variables in this matter.

Where techniques are described later in this book the term 'right' or 'left' rudder is used. This means that the wheel is turned to the right thereby turning the barge to starboard or to left to go to port. 'Hard over' means turning the wheel to its maximum useful or available angle.

Rudders on older barges are large, having evolved from those on sailing ships. This feature continued through into the early iron barges which were built for sail – allowing the barge to be steered whilst moving at low speeds without the aid of thrust onto the rudder. As engines were introduced into barges the thrust from the propeller resulted in rudders becoming more efficient, making it possible to have a smaller blade. Shorter rudders were easier to handle, took up less space in locks and docks and made steering lighter work.

Position of the Rudder on the Barge.

The position of the rudder relative to the propeller and its surface area are critical and it is the combination of these two elements that determines how a motor barge steers. The siting of the rudder will depend on the type of barge. For instance, old sailing barges have a long rudder pivoted on the sternpost. More modern, and purpose-built, motor barges have the rudder (or rudders) located under the counter. This saves space in the footprint the barge has on the water and works well with the high thrust of a fast revving engine. But these barges won't steer well whilst drifting when out of gear. You need to maintain enough propulsion to make the rudder effective ('steerage way').

Hull Shape & Rudder

How well the water flows past the hull to the rudder will be affected by the hull shape. Fine old sailing ship hulls will deliver a smooth flow whereas the big, lumpy commercial barges use power from the props to create steerage. This gives different characteristics to the handling of each type.

Rudder Angle

Rudders are only efficient within an angle of 35 degrees each side of centre. After this point the useful effect reduces. However you may still want the facility to fold your rudder flat against the transom to save space when moored.

See **Part Four: Rudder Types.**

BITTS & BOLLARDS

Bitts are a pair of vertical posts for securing rope to; a bollard is a single vertical post.

On each side your barge should be fitted with a pair of large bitts at the fore deck and either a single bollard or pair of bitts on the stern depending on the size of your barge. These should be securely attached to the ship. This is an area where, in older ships, there can often be rot either in the bitt or the surrounding steelwork. If the bitts haven't been filled with oil or cement they may well be rotting from the inside as well. Make sure they are sound because your barge may need to hang on them. The pins set into a bitt are also important. There should

be three on each post. The top two will be opposite each other and the third should be on the outer edge, lower and slightly round the bitt. These are there to run the rope around, keep it separated and stop it crossing over itself and thereby jamming. Depending on your type of barge, there may also be a large single bitt (bollard) with two pins on the centre at the aft end. On the fore deck, if you don't have a suitably strong anchor winch, you may also want a bollard or samson post. You will notice that on commercial barges the

bitts are quite large. This is important since you may be running ropes up to 36mm around them up to four times. Little bitts may be neater on deck but they are of limited use to you. There should also be a pair of bitts at a convenient point outside the wheelhouse door so that the helmsman can leap into action with his cunningly prepared shorter rope. On barges with a large aft cabin these may replace the aftermost bitts due to lack of working deck space. In addition to this your barge will be considerably easier to manage if you install either small bitts or cleats along the side. Ideally they should be placed about one third in from each end and also one in the middle. This should be roughly in line with your pivot point. These are vital for certain warping techniques and for single-handed working. They make life much easier when you are working downstream and need a fixed point other than the ends of the barge.

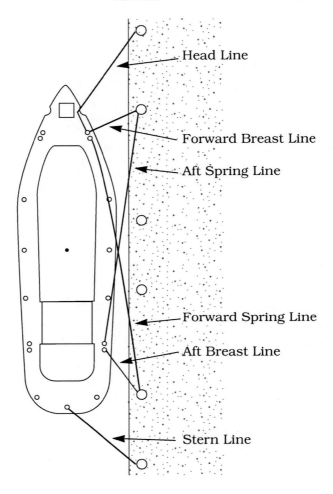

Head Line

Forward Breast Line

Aft Spring Line

Forward Spring Line

Aft Breast Line

Stern Line

Fairleads

Fairleads are designed to lead ropes 'fair' in the right direction across the sides of the barge. They may be needed at bow and stern, depending on the design of your barge, and protect both spring and head lines so you may need more than one at each end. They can be located on the top of the gunwale or you can use a ring welded into the side to run through. If you have good bitts on the barge then fairleads may not be needed if the line runs cleanly ashore. When the barge is moored up for any length of time, it is worth protecting the ropes from chafing by putting some plastic hose round them where they pass through the fairlead or over sharp or rough edges.

Part Two

BARGE HANDLING

This section looks at some techniques for handling a barge and some ideas on how to do it more successfully. With over 25 years experience of driving barges – two of my own and many others – I still look forward at every trip to facing new challenges and working out how to get the ship to manoeuvre successfully.

THE MAJOR FORCES

The movement of any vessel is controlled or affected by three major forces. Current, Wind and Engine.

The first two have been providing power for quite a long time for everything from sailing ships to wind and watermills. The engine is a newer idea.

Given that your barge is sitting in liquid, it is going to be subjected to any number of factors which can affect its movement. The barge may be small or large but it weighs many tonnes and it is astonishing how easy it is to make it move, often in a way you would rather it didn't.

Currents & Tidal Streams

These may vary from a nominal flow in canals to an enormous force in tidal water or a river. Fast moving waters will throw the barge round before you know it. They are a powerful and valuable motive force when used to your advantage. They may be running at or near the margins of your barge's speed so knowledge of local conditions is vital. Most barges will make between 5 and 7 knots through the water. Tidal streams can run at anything from 1/2 to 4 knots; rivers can run even faster. The tidal Ouse and Trent (UK) can run at up to 9 knots. Calculate these into your plans or you may be going backwards.

Wind

When it is blowing hard the wind is just as potent as the other two forces and if it is blowing that hard you probably shouldn't be venturing forth. Insurers draw the line at anything above Force 4 when you go to sea. Most of the time the wind will be the gentlest of the three but this doesn't mean it won't be effective. Anyone who has stuck the nose of their barge out of a sheltered dock will know how the bow can be pushed round. Again a helpful force when used to your advantage. Both wind speed and direction should be accounted for in calculating your movements .

Engine(s)

A barge is generally fitted with one main engine. Bow thrusters are an auxiliary source of power but, for the purpose of learning how to handle your barge, they have been taken out of the equation in this book.

The thrust from the engine is the main mechanical force over which you have absolute control. The 'drive train' consisting of engine, gearbox and clutch, shaft and propeller, needs to be understood, respected and kept in good order. Generally speaking barges are fitted with engines ranging from 85 to 220hp. Lower than 85hp can be perfectly acceptable for smaller barges or those which have very fine lines and move easily through the water. At the top end of the scale you may want a powerful engine to get you across the channel or up the Rhone or Rhine, for example. But most barges are operating in relatively quiet canals and the top end size, designed to move fully laden barges, rarely gets used to optimum performance. Idling along with a big engine can cause glazing of the cylinder bores resulting in a lot of smoke. Whilst this book advocates that manoeuvres be done slowly there are also times when you need to apply a lot of engine power to drive yourself out of trouble.

Using the Drive Train

On modern engines the usual method of controlling engine and gearbox is by a single lever control. With the lever upright, the throttle is in idle and the gear is not engaged. Moving to the first position, either forwards or backwards, engages the gear direction but does not increase the engine revs. By slowly advancing the lever the revs will be increased and the ship will start to move. Getting the correct setting for engine revs in the 'idle' position is important for barge handling. If the tickover is too slow then the engine will stall. If it is too high then the engine produces too much thrust and you speed up too quickly and do not have the ability to go slowly enough. Too high a tickover can also damage the gearbox clutches. Single lever controls can be adjusted to ensure that the gear has engaged before the engine revs are increased.

The throttle should always be moved slowly to allow engine revs to build up or fall away without stress. Remember that this little lever is sending a message to a massive piece of moving machinery. It is creating huge amounts of energy and force: moving too dramatically, especially from full ahead to full astern, may well cause damage to gears, engine mounts or the shaft and flexible drive coupling. The engine needs enough time to slow down.

This rule is particularly important for engines which have separate controls for gear and throttle. Always engage the gear before increasing the revs and, as ever, do it gently. You will get a better response from your propeller by doing this since a crash change of direction only sets up a flurry of cavitation rather than a 'bite' in the water. Even if you are faced with an impending crisis most barge movements happen relatively slowly so don't let the panic in your brain overtake the use of controls. This will be a time when you can least afford to lose your motive power.

In some rare cases you may come across a direct-reversing engine. These don't have a gearbox and have to be stopped and re-started in the opposite direction to go backwards. Handling a barge with one of these is an art in itself and it would be advisable to take lessons from an experienced skipper before trying it.

TIP: Single lever controls are better for less experienced skippers.

THE MINOR FORCES

Inertia

This is included here because the sheer weight of the mass of a barge moving through the water becomes a 'Force' in itself. It must be taken into account when calculating the movement and drift of the barge. When the barge is travelling round a bend, its own weight will carry it (centrifugal force) towards the outside of the curve.

Currents, Swirls, Eddies and Oxbows

Reading the movement and direction of the water is an essential skill in barge handling. This is when you are glad you remember everything you learnt in Geography about oxbows. The deeper and faster water is always on the outside of a bend. Correspondingly you should steer clear of the shallows on the inside of the bend. In canals there is a minefield of swirls and back currents at every dock and lock entrance. Weirs also have a pull of water in their direction to be considered. This applies as you approach a lock where the weir is next to it. They should be considered as forces which can have an effect on how the barge moves.

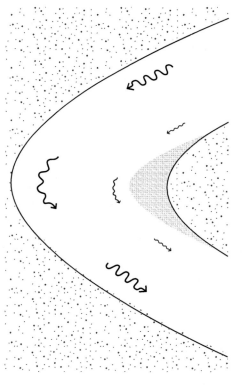

See **Running Downstream**.

Bargees familiar with the Thames and the entrance to Limehouse Basin will know how the tide is trying to move you in one direction but the minute you put your bow into the lock entrance it gets bumped against the wall by the back eddy swirling around the gates.

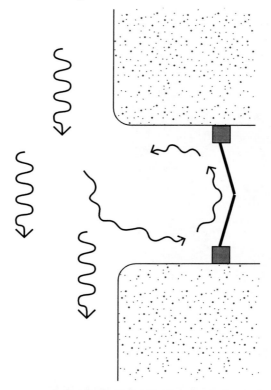

TIP There are many clues available to the skipper on the surface of the water. Leaves or other surface debris will be evidence of slack water or a returning eddy.

Remember that you have the maximum control of your barge when heading up into the stream and the wind. When these are on the beam they will have an effect on your course and you will be swept or blown sideways. You have the least control when they are astern since you will be carried along by them.

Demonstrating the need for a rope on the bucket.

Blokzijl, St Jean de Losne, France. This collapsible wheelhouse has good side door access as well as double doors opening on to the aft deck.

TECHNIQUES – How To Do It

You don't actually 'drive' a barge. In spite of that deceptive wheel it is not on rails, it is adrift. 'Driving' the barge is about controlling how it swings through the water. The key to this is to anticipate, by reading the situation and using the forces, where the barge will swing next and counteracting it before it happens. Propeller rotation will gently steer a barge off in one direction or the other so you will constantly be correcting this to maintain a straight course. Generally speaking if you start the barge turning by putting the wheel over then you will need to start correcting the swing by applying a little turn back again. If you wait until you reach the desired position, it will have swung too far. You will have to work hard to get out of the zigzag and back on a straight course. Again, it is easier to apply small amounts of turn or return and keep adding to the movement than it is to put too much into it too soon. It is amazing to discover just how delicate and sensitive this great lump of iron can be if it isn't pushed around too radically. Having mastered the art of controlling the drift, you can think about using it to advantage. You can, for example, set up a situation where you allow a calculated drift to take you into a mooring or to line you up for a bridge hole. This is not like a car which, if you take your hands off the wheel, goes straight.

Relative Bearing Angle

Remember that, although you may be positioning the barge in the direction you want to arrive at, the combination of all the forces may dictate that you arrive 'off line'. This means that your bow is pointing in one direction while the barge is drifting in another. This is the concept of Steady Relative Bearing Angle which will bring you, by design, to the right place. Another vessel closing on a constant relative bearing angle to yours may collide with you even though it is pointing in a different direction. This is essentially a technique used at sea to find out whether you are going to collide.

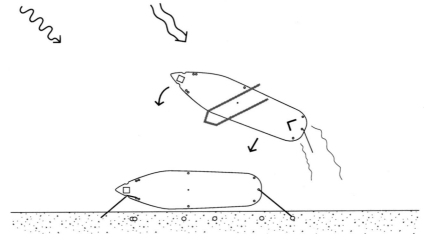

Waterways: Inland and Tidal

Differing approaches are required depending on the type of waterway you are using. If you are cruising on canals and inland rivers you will experience quieter conditions (unless there are floods).

This is how most leisure bargees will spend their time. All the approaches to barge handling described in this book apply to inland waters.

Tidal waters, however, dictate rules of their own. Most bargees will plan their journeys to have the tide running with them. You will cover ground a lot faster this way saving time and energy. Unless you have a very powerful engine, pushing against a contrary tide is slow and tiring work.

Since the tide can carry you along so fast virtually all

manoeuvres need to be carried out with the bow heading up into the stream. This is the only way you have control of the situation. Coming into a mooring, picking up a mooring buoy, ferry gliding or waiting for a lock to open must be done with your bow heading up to the tidal stream. This also applies when you are leaving a mooring unless you have a clear run downstream in front of you and can take a flying start (also see page 34). Since tides turn every six and a quarter hours (approx) there is always a period of slack water around the top and bottom of the tidal range. This usually lasts for about half an hour as the tide slows down, stops and then turns to run in the opposite direction. This is a useful time for doing things like turning the barge round on the mooring (which might be helpful when you want to depart).

If you are operating in tidal or strong river waters then you should compute these elements into your manoeuvres.

Get to Know Your Barge

Before you start anything you should learn how your barge actually moves through the water. Your understanding of this is the first part of the equation for good handling. If possible find a stretch of water which is quiet and gives plenty of space to move around. A dock or a basin off the canal can be ideal and there won't be too many other vessels moving about. The first thing to do is locate your pivot point. With the barge stationary in the middle of the water put the wheel over to one side and give a short burst of power. The stern will move over, the bow will come round and you can identify the axis point. Again from a stationary postion do the same thing going astern which will show the effect of your prop walk. You can practise these moves with increasing degrees of power to see the difference it makes. You can also, starting at one end of the dock, put on a bit of speed and then take it out of gear to see how far it travels. If you do this and then turn the rudder half way down the dock you will see how the barge drifts ahead sideways on its own inertia while pivoting and turning at the same time. Try turning to port and to starboard to see the difference. Once you have achieved this understanding of barge movement you can progress to a waterway with a light stream running. This will allow you to experience the effect of a current on your bow and how it can move the barge from side to side. Try this while holding a stationary position in the middle of the waterway. **Turning Round** and **Ferry Gliding** are looked at in more detail in their own sections.

LEAVING A MOORING

OBJECTIVE get the barge to move away from the mooring without scraping the side
FACTORS stream, wind, other vessels
CHECK fenders positioned, crew onboard and briefed

The first rule is to move the pivot point of the barge away from the side. This will allow you to steer the bow out without hitting the stern against the bank.

Pointing Upstream

This should be the easy bit. Having considered the effect of all the forces let us assume that there are no excessive elements at play and nothing in front of you. With the spring lines taken off you are now 'singled up' with just a bow and stern line secured. Cast off, apply a small but increasing amount of power (thrust) and the barge can be steered off the berth. If you are moving upstream you can use the current to push the bow out into the stream.

However you may need more than this to achieve the effect.

Forward Spring

The next way of getting a barge to move off is by keeping the bow line secure and driving forward against it. With the wheel over, the bow will tuck in and the stern will come away from the bank. The pivot point is now moved sideways away from the wall. Cast off, put the wheel over, apply forward gear and the barge will pivot round – pointing the bow out to the stream without bumping the aft end or damaging the prop.

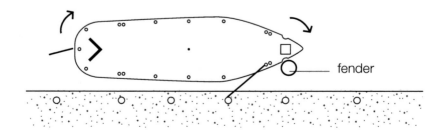

fender

Aft Spring

An alternative is to secure a short spring to the aft bitts and go astern. The barge will screw round, without moving backwards, and the bow will be brought away from the wall. This simple trick removes the need for a bow thruster. This is ideal if you are in a berth with several large barges each end of you. It may be the only way you can drive out forwards. You should have good big fenders on the aft corner to keep your prop and rudder away from damage on the wall. This technique won't work so well if you have either current or strong wind pinning you against the wall.

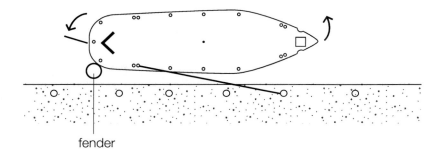

fender

Angelus using the aft spring to come away from the wall.

Leaving a Mooring : Example 1

In this situation the barge must get off the mooring by reversing downstream and round the end of the island. Prop walk pulls the barge to port.

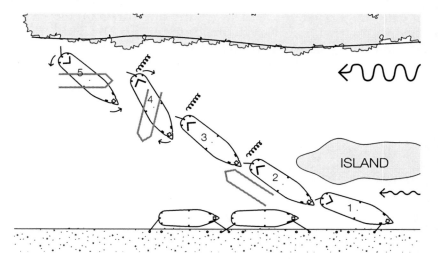

1. Keeping the bow spring on, motor forward to get the stern out to an angle of about 35 degrees.

2. Minor current pushes the barge sideways as reverse gear is engaged. Prop walk (to port) will start to pull the barge round the end of the island.

3. As the stern comes into the main stream the aft end will be pushed sideways by the stronger current.

4. From this position forward gear can now be engaged and the wheel put over to turn and head downstream.

5. To head upstream: the barge is allowed to go further back before engaging forward gear and left rudder to bring the head up to the stream.

Leaving a Mooring : Example 2

This illustrates what happens if the barge has a prop walk to starboard.

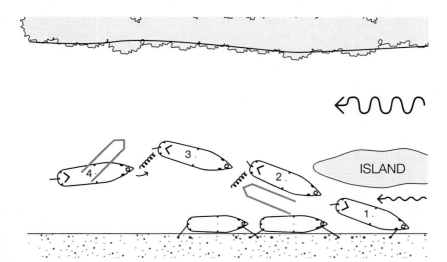

1. Keeping the bow line on, motor the barge forward to get the stern out to an angle of about 45 degrees.

2. Minor current pushes the ship sideways as reverse gear is engaged. Prop walk (to starboard) starts to pull the barge back and straightens her up.

3   Prop walk and major current continue to take the barge astern. In this position you can engage forward gear and left rudder to move upstream past the island.

4   If heading downstream allow the barge to continue further back before engaging forward gear and hard left rudder to spin round the pivot point. As the barge turns round the major current will help to push the bow round.

Pointing Downstream

Leaving a mooring with a slight stream coming down behind can be done as already described but a significant stream will present more of a challenge and there are a number of options. One option is to turn the barge round on the mooring with the use of ropes so that you have the advantage of pointing into the stream. With a line round from the outside of the bow to the upstream end of the berth, and a little engine power, you can spin the barge round hauling the bow line in. However you must have planned where you can turn the barge again if you want to continue your journey downstream.

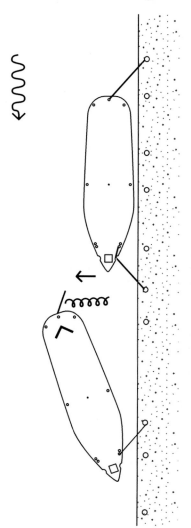

Another option (illustrated here) is to drive forward against the spring thereby moving the aft end off the mooring and then go astern. Consideration must be made for the effect of prop walk. Depending on the rotation you may get more or less help. It can be the case that a prop walk which ostensibly brings you back into the berth will actually help prevent the stern being taken too far out. Rope can prevent you going too far.

This should not be attempted if the stream is very strong and could whip your stern round.

CAUTION! Remember you always have less control if you are pointing downstream.

RUNNING DOWNSTREAM

OBJECTIVE manage the barge with stream behind
FACTORS speed of current, wind
CHECK stern anchors prepared

With the stream behind you, you are potentially a victim of the forces at work. Working downstream requires more forward thinking and anticipation. You must allow more space because your increased speed will carry you further.

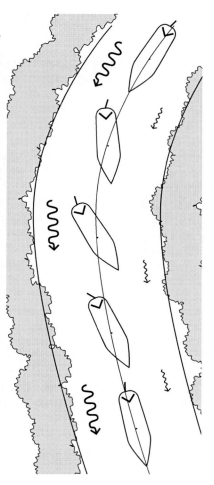

Although it is exhilarating to gallop along at a rate of knots you are, to some degree, out of control. The barge will drift and swing happily into the bends more than usual so make sure you have allowed compensation for this in good time. More than a few people have been caught out and unceremoniously deposited into the trees on the outside of the bend.

In mainland Europe this is where the Blue Flag is often encountered. A vessel travelling upstream may be choosing a course closest to the inside of the bends in order to minimise the effect of the current.

TIP: As you take the corner, put the bow towards the inside of the bend and let the stream push the aft end round before you straighten up.

BRIDGE HOLES

OBJECTIVE pass through the bridge without hitting it, the bank or another vessel
FACTORS direction of current, wind
CHECK other vessels, hazards on either side of the bridge.

Passing through bridges illustrates how to use the pivot point. Most skippers will entertain themselves by trying to get the barge to go exactly through the centre of the arch. Eventually this will become a subconcious action on your part and it is easily done on a straight stretch of water. However rivers tend to be less obliging than long straight canals and the bridges are often situated on or near a bend. This means that you will need to swing or drift the barge into or out of the bridge hole. You will quickly learn just how far your barge is going to sideslip when it turns. The trick when approaching a narrow bridge hole at an angle is to allow enough of the bow to enter the hole, wait for the pivot point to arrive outside the hole and then put the wheel over, give a burst of power and push the aft end round into line. Because the barge pivots this will bring the bow, which was about to hit the bridge side, back into line and you will glide cleanly through the bridge without touching the sides. In order to reduce sideslip it is important to approach the bridge slowly. As you move through the bridge you can apply more power to push the aft end back into line. Bridges which have a sharp bend on the other side present a slight variation on this technique. You will need to start swinging the bow across in the direction of the bend even as you are entering the bridge hole. The pivot point should be aimed through at an angle and, as you come through, you will need to apply power to push the barge on and round the bend. However, in doing this, you will now find that the aft end is swinging into the bank. Having got this far at a suitably dignified speed you may now need to apply opposite rudder and a burst of power to push the aft end away from the shore.

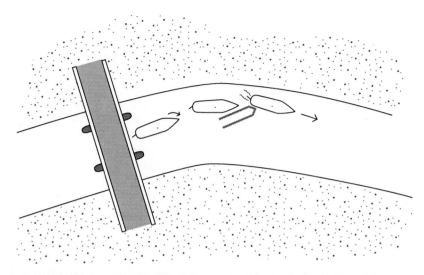

TIP: Heading upstream gives you good control and is easier than downstream. When the current is astern (from behind you) allow more space to line up and compensate for additional drift.

TIP: Remember that the vessel travelling with the current has right of way. This is particularly important at narrow bridges where you may have to 'stand off' until the vessel with right of way has cleared through.

CAUTION: In strong stream conditions the water will pile up at very narrow bridge holes. If you are going upstream, this will slow you down and put extra pressure on your bow. If you are going downstream, however, this can be quite exhilerating.

TIP: Make sure you have all the relevant dimensions of air draught and the width of your wheelhouse roof as well as those of the bridges you are encountering.

Advanced Technique

Navigating downstream through some bridges in very strong current conditions may need a different approach. This involves going through backwards. If a bridge is quite narrow or situated near a bend this may be the only way to get through without smashing the barge into either the bridge or the bank. This is probably a trick for the more experienced skipper but the principle is simple. You have control of a barge which is head up to the current. Line the ship up above the bridge heading away from it. Ease off the throttle slowly until you are being carried slowly backwards by the stream. Maintain sufficient revs to keep your bow head up and make sure you keep the barge central to the bridge hole. Make sure that the stream doesn't push the bow round which can happen very quickly. If you have any problems you still have the option of applying full power and taking yourself back upstream and clear of the bridge. The point is that you are always in charge of what is happening. Being smashed sideways through a bridge going downstream is not fun.

CAUTION!: Do not rely on a bow thruster to hold you central. However, if you do and it fails at the critical moment, you should still be able to drive upstream and out of the bridge.

Very Advanced Technique

Another interesting variation on passing through bridges occurs when the air draught of the bridge is slightly too low. You may have noticed, when you apply more power, that the stern digs deeper into the water and the bow correspondingly lifts up. This can be used to dip under low bridges. Approach the bridge at speed, take off the power and the bow will dip down. As you pass into the bridge hole apply full power again and the stern will bite deep taking you through in a dipping swoop. Commercial ships in mainland Europe use this trick when running empty without cargo. Sometimes they put water into the hold which rushes to the fore end when slowing down and then back aft when full power is applied. This manoeuvre takes considerable nerve and experience. It is recommended that you don't try this in your own home. Wheelhouses are very expensive to replace.

A simpler version of this technique is to creep slowly up the bridge and get as much weight as possible on the fore end. Move the bow through and then transfer all the extra weight to the stern. Using lots of people for this is the best way because they will move themselves.

TIP: Remember to lower your mast. Many masts, both tall and short, have met their fate at a bridge. When you have been moored up for a few days, with the mast up, it is all too easy to forget to lower it. Add this to your pre-departure check list.

OFF-CENTRE BRIDGE APPROACH

Here the problem is that the bridge is quite close to the lock. Only the centre arch is available for passage and there is a considerable stream running down from the weir.

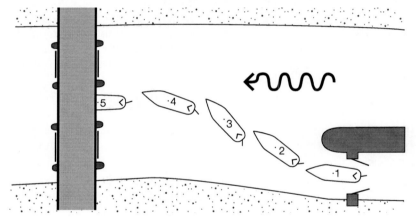

1   Exit the lock and put on hard right rudder.

2   Steer the barge close round the end of the lock wall.

3   Continue forward until the stream starts to push the bow round and your bow is approaching the centre line for the arch.

4   Put the rudder hard over to port and apply a strong burst of power. Pivot the barge round and line up for the arch.

5   Apply right rudder to correct the swing, straighten up and head down through the bridge.

TIP: Remember that the downstream vessel has right of way.

MOORING

OBJECTIVE come alongside, tie up, prepare for departure
FACTORS stream, wind, prop walk, drift
CHECK other vessels moored, moving or likely to move

Before you moor it is very important to calculate what you will need to do when you leave. Getting tied up in the direction of travel may make it difficult to get out later. Consideration should be given to possible effects of stream, tide, wind, space to manoeuvre, what vessels are there now and what may be there later when you want to depart. Consider the effect your propeller is going to have. Prop walk, used correctly, will be helpful but if it is acting against you it can negate all your efforts. Think about what effect you want when going astern. It may well pay to turn the barge round before going alongside. This can apply even if you think you want to carry on in the same direction later. There are more 'embarrassing moments' caused by barges trying to get out than by any other manoeuvre. This is also a time when a softly, softly technique may be more effective than attempting to apply huge amounts of revs to power your way out.

If you are running downstream in a strong current you must turn and head into the current before mooring up or you will be carried past the berth at speed.

As a general rule, when approaching a mooring even if it is familiar to you, you should slow right down and see what effect the stream and wind are having on the barge. This will vary every time and you need to 'feel' how the barge is being moved. Then you can calculate whether you will be helped or hindered by the other forces. It may be that the wind or stream will push you gently into your berth or you may need a different strategy to moor up successfully.

TIP: By selecting two or more fixed marks, Transit Points, on the shore you can line up the position of the barge relative to your intended mooring. This will show whether you need to move forward, drop back or move sideways.
See Ferry Gliding p51

With Kick

'Kick' means the direction your prop walk will take the aft end when going astern.

As you come alongside to moor, the direction of paddle wheel will affect the way in which you approach. Assuming that the stern pulls to port when going astern, then a port side mooring should be approached at an angle

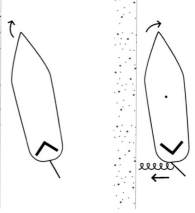

keeping the stern away from the wall and aiming the bow up to the wall at the point just short of where you wish to stop. By going astern the aft end will tuck into the wall as the bow eases away. You will now lay alongside nicely. This manoeuvre can be refined with practice. As you aim towards your designated point, you can come out of gear and allow the barge to drift forward. By subtle application of gentle reverse and forward gears you can 'wiggle' the barge into a good position by the time you have drifted up to the wall.

Against Kick

This means the opposite direction to that of the prop walk.

Mooring on the other side is not so easy. If you put the bow into the wall then the stern will be taken further away when you reverse. This will put you at an unhelpful angle. Here the trick is to steer the barge into a gentle arc away from the side allowing the stern to swing into the wall. By applying reverse before the stern hits the side

you will paddle the aft end away from the wall which will bring the bow back into the side. This manoeuvre is not as easy as the other side and will take more practice to judge it correctly. With experience you will be able to lay the barge alongside easily allowing crew to get lines ashore, or yourself if single handed, without any commotion. Again, you can apply calculated drift and wiggle to the move.

Securing

With the bow neatly alongside the trick is to get a bow or stern line secured ashore quickly. In the first instant you need to have control of the bow but should allow enough slack on the rope to permit the stern to be brought in. If you make it fast on a short line too quickly the barge will be prevented from swinging in. By taking a couple of turns round the bitts you can slacken or tighten the rope until the helmsman is satisfied that the stern is in place.

Always secure the upstream end of the barge first even if this happens to be the stern. The flow of current will push the other end into the bank.

TIP: When making off the springs, having secured the first one, use the engine to drive the ship against it and then secure the other one. This is easier than attempting to haul in tight by hand.

TIP: Travelling through the Netherlands, and looking for some-where to tie up, I found that many commercial skippers are happy to have you alongside if you have an historic barge. They call them 'our Grandfathers' ships'. Avoid invading their privacy, try not to put your wheelhouse opposite theirs, walk over on the foredeck, and be prepared to move quickly. A few strong 'Leffe' beers go down well, too.

TURNING ROUND

OBJECTIVE turn the ship in the minimum space
FACTORS prop walk, current speed and direction, wind
CHECK space available, bankside hazards, moving vessels, alternative strategies

A barge standing still in dead water will turn round its pivot point without gaining very much forward movement. Hard over with the rudder and some short, sharp and hard bursts of thrust will kick the stern around. You will turn in not much more than your own length. If you have space to get round in one move then turn in the same direction as your prop walk since prop rotation will give you a tighter circle. More often than not, space will be restricted and the manoeuvre will need several back and forth movements to get you round. This is sometimes called 'back and fill'. Ideally you should choose the direction of the turn so that your prop walk, when reversing, will pull the stern to the outer edge of your turning circle thereby assisting the manoeuvre. You don't need to do a lot of frantic wheel turning. Once the wheel is set over for the required direction it can stay there. Prop walk will do half the job and rudder deflection will help. The object of the exercise is to get the bow round without gaining ground. Again short but

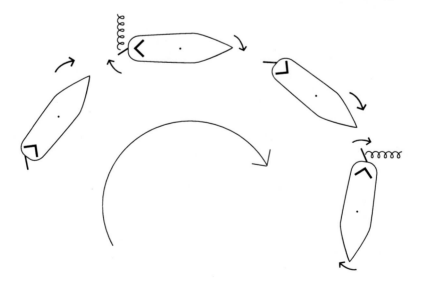

hard bursts are what is needed. This pushes the aft end round without allowing time for the barge to start moving forward.

Other techniques for turning your ship are to put the bow (protected with a good barge fender) gently against the shore or wharf, then motor the stern round. A spud leg or lee board can be used to create a sort of anchor effect or use ropes if you can get a line ashore. If you have sufficient space to get the barge round in one single move it may help to turn the bow into the strongest element of available current. This may mean turning in the opposite direction to the one dictated by prop walk but a strong current will push you round more readily.

TIP: If possible always start a turn from a near stationary position. If you are travelling downstream this will be more difficult but do what you can to prevent being swept down too far. If you are moving forward and you engage reverse gear to slow the barge, your prop walk will start pivoting the barge round before you have actually stopped thereby assisting the manouevre

CAUTION: If turning upstream of a bridge – which is generally not a good plan – make sure that you have allowed sufficient sea room to complete the move. If you are too close, the current may carry you beam on into the bridge.

CAUTION: Never turn close to a blind bend. You can't see what might be coming.

Many years ago, on my first barge, I was riding the tide up the Thames to Richmond. My plan was to turn the barge and come alongside the wall head up to the tide. There was considerable wind behind me. I misjudged the speed of both tide and wind and was carried much further upstream than I planned. This brought me on to a collision course with the passenger trip boat lying on the berth further upstream. At this point I had no option but attempt to complete the turn since I was being carried upstream beam on. A collision was inevitable. In order to minimise the impact I allowed the stern to swing round towards the trip boat. Shortly before impact I put the rudder hard over and gave a full burst of power. This drove my stern away from the other boat. The impact was minimised and the only damage was a burst fender – oh, and my pride, of course. The trip boat skipper still waves to me. On this occasion I had not allowed enough space for the strength of the wind pushing me upstream.

Turning off a mooring using the stream

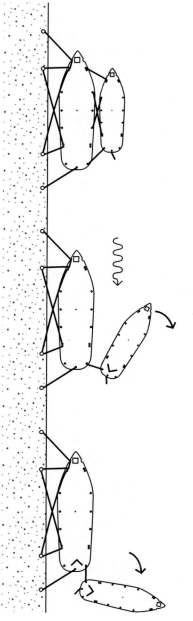

LOCKING

OBJECTIVE pass through professionally and efficiently
FACTORS stream, wind, prop walk
CHECK other vessels using the lock

Heading Upstream

A lock which is being filled is a more lively place than an emptying one. Surges may come from either end so be prepared. If the lock fills from the sides or bottom the chamber will be much calmer. There are different approaches to how locks should be worked. On the Thames, for example, it is the custom to secure the vessel at bow and stern and ease the ropes as the level changes. The engine must be turned off unless you have the lock to yourself. It is not permitted to sit on a single forward spring with the engine running on tickover. However this is standard practice in mainland Europe. In France the Freycinet (Peniche size) locks are more conducive to the average pleasure barge. The very big commercial waterway locks have floating bollards rising and falling in the wall. These may be too far apart to do anything other than secure to only one bollard and use the engine to hold the barge in position.

Heading Downstream

Yes, you guessed it. Down stream locks may have some degree of current running into them. You will almost certainly be using reverse gear to slow and stop the barge but, because of the prop walk, the stern is going to one side or the other. Depending on which side you kick astern, and whatever else may be happening in the lock, it works if you use a middle to aft end line. This will prevent the stern from being thrown round when the barge comes to a halt. The same trick for easing the line round the bitt will gently brake the barge and she'll lay into the wall. As the lock empties the line(s) should be eased off the bitt without getting locked on. This is where the pins can be used to route the rope round without crossing over itself. There can't be many bargees who haven't got a rope snagged on the bitts in a falling lock. They may, of course, not admit it. Keep a razor-sharp knife or axe immediately accessible. When it happened to me I had the axe out and the rope cut in a twinkling. Cut the line across the edge of the top of the bitt like a scissor action. If you are cutting through a spliced eye choose the end which has been worked in. This will reduce your losses slightly and the rope can be re-spliced. Beware of trying to cut the line somewhere along its length with an axe. It may bounce so use the knife and watch out for whiplash.

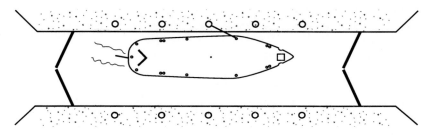

CAUTION: An interesting phenomenon to be aware of is this. A lock emptying itself downstream may, if the next lock is close, send a surge of water back up the canal again. This can create an unexpected force on your bow and even lift you a few centimetres. We know of one case where a wheelhouse got damaged under a bridge by this occurrence.

CAUTION: A common cause of 'hang up' in locks happens if you have a line looped up around the bollard on the lock side. If the lock is deep a loop will be easier to retrieve than trying to flick an eye off a high bollard. You simply pull the loose end round and back to the barge. But if you allow the rope to cross over itself on the edge of the lock side, the free end rope may be trapped under the weight of the other part as the ship descends. Never allow ropes to cross over. Make sure they can run freely.

STOPPING – Mid-stream

OBJECTIVE   stop the barge in the middle of the waterway
without twisting round off course
FACTORS   current speed and direction, prop walk, wind
CHECK   other vessels nearby, especially behind

This is a 'controlling chaos' moment. For starters this
enormous hulk is going to carry on regardless. Depending on
the steering qualities of your particular rudder, you should
slow the barge down as early as possible knowing that it is
easy to put more power on. If you need to stop quickly you
will be going astern with the engine. Your prop walk will now
slew the barge round at an angle. In order to stop in a straight
line the trick is to steer off at an angle first so that the
reversing prop walk will then slew the barge back on to your
course line. Depending on the situation you may elect to
reposition the line of the barge before you do this by moving
over to one side or the other. This will allow more space to pull
off the trick.

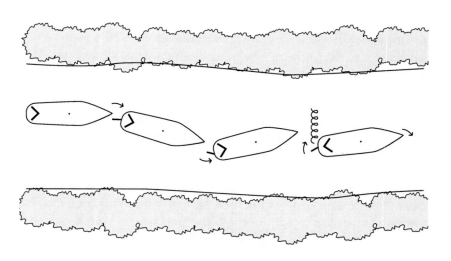

HOLDING STATION

OBJECTIVE keep stationary midstream while waiting for lock, bridge or other traffic

FACTORS current speed and direction, prop walk, wind

CHECK other moving vessels, alternative strategy

This is sometimes referred to as 'Standing Off' which says what it means. Whilst waiting for a lock or a moveable bridge you have the challenge of keeping your barge in a stationary position This is very much a case where you have to think of all the main forces. With no engine power, the barge becomes very prone to the effects of both wind and current. If you think you are getting into this position plan ahead by slowing down early. This will give you more manoeuvring space. Now you can apply the principles of back and fill (*see* **Turning Round**) using all the forces and also using the effect you can achieve by going astern. If the area is free of wind and current then it will be quite easy to keep the barge on station by going a little forward and then reversing the prop walk to go back to where you came from. If you have wind or stream behind you this manoeuvre becomes more difficult so allow extra space. You may have to consider turning round and head up to the prevailing force. This will give you control of the barge until you are ready to move on.

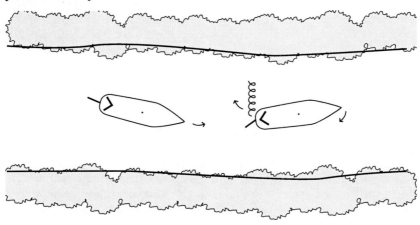

REMEMBER. You always have control when head up to stream and wind. When these are abeam or astern your barge will be carried by them.

REVERSING

OBJECTIVE go backwards in a straight line
FACTORS current speed and direction, prop walk, wind
CHECK other moving vessels, bankside hazards

This is one of the most challenging manoeuvres for most bargees. Is it possible? Most people will tell you that steering a barge going backwards doesn't happen. It will propwalk itself off to the side quite cheerfully. Having said that, it can be done. This manoeuvre takes a lot of practice and needs very calm conditions. The trick is to set the rudder angle a few degrees off centre on the opposite side to the prop walk. Acting as a deflector, not a rudder, it will help to ease the barge off to that side. The balancing act is to get exactly the right revs astern to counter the rudder deflection. (Too high revs will set up turbulence making it more difiicult.) When you have achieved this, the ship may go back in a straight line. Do not change the engine speed when you've got it right. You'll upset the balance and veer off to one side. The longer the ship, the easier this is since the hull itself acts as a straight rudder.

If you can't manage this then go to plan B. Set up the angle of the barge before going astern so you can use the prop walk to straighten it up again. In still water this can be repeated again and again until you reach the desired position. Patience, and slow revs, are what are needed. The effect of prop walk can be reduced by giving short bursts of power only at a time which prevents the 'walk' from developing. Also, if you have a large rudder, it can be set at a slight angle to deflect the stern generally in the required direction – with luck.

Other techniques include dragging some kind of weight such as a towed dinghy, sea anchor, large rope, light chain, pole or whatever comes to hand to create drag on the same side as the prop walk. This will help to stop the bow swinging round the pivot point. However, if you moor at the end of a long blind alley and the only way out is backwards, then this is the time to install a bow thruster. This is the one manoeuvre where it really comes into its own. Whether it is worth the money for this alone is a moot point. How many times will you need to reverse significantly enough to justify the expense?

TIP: If you are trying this in shallow water, the rudder may have a better steering effect than when in deeper water.

FERRY GLIDING

OBJECTIVE   slot neatly into tight berth, cross waterway
sideways
FACTORS   current speed and direction, wind
CHECK   moving vessels

This is one of the most satisfying and rewarding tricks. The
barge can be made to move completely sideways across the
waterway without losing or gaining ground. However it does
need help from one of the forces. You need to be head up to a
current – or a good wind – to do the pushing and in this
manoeuvre this will be the dominant force. The engine is used
simply to ensure that the barge holds station as it crosses the
waterway. Make sure that the current doesn't throw the bow
round or you will be going down the road beam on. So you
can cross the river from one side to the other very easily. It
will also drop the ship neatly into a tight mooring and you
don't need more than a few centimetres at each end to get in.
It is deeply impressive. Expect applause.

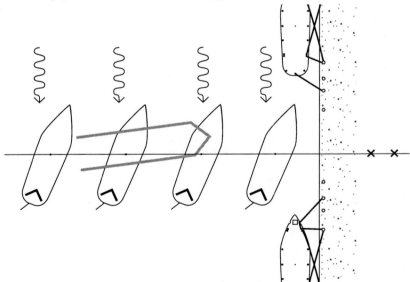

If there is no current or stream available to push you across
then this manoeuvre can be achieved by using the 'wiggle'
trick. Essentially you simply drive straight across and then
wiggle around the pivot point as though you were coming
alongside in a lock.

SHIP TO SHIP MOVEMENTS

The Vacuum Effect

A barge under way pushes the water in front thereby creating an area of force. As the water passes down the side the force reduces. When it reaches the stern it comes together to fill the void left by the vessel moving forwards. It's a bit like the tsunami effect in miniature. The first big wave creates a hole which then tries to refill from both directions. Then the next wave comes along and it happens again. In open water this isn't a problem. But if you are in a very narrow or shallow area of water the changes, when travelling at speed, won't have time to equate. This simply creates a vacuum effect and the barge is pulled towards the bank. Do not attempt to apply more power to get away. As ever the 'do it slowly' rule comes into play and, by easing off the power, the situation can be retrieved. The same applies to very shallow waters. Narrow lock cut approaches are a good example of where this problem manifests itself.

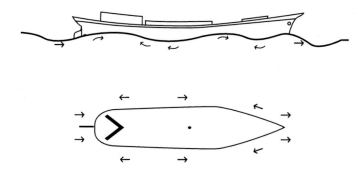

TIP: Look over your shoulder when moving down a narrow waterway or close to the shore. If your following wave is breaking along the bank then you are travelling too fast. Slow down, let the water pressures equate and you'll see the wake become a ripple instead of a wave.

TIP: Keep looking behind you. A large vehicle mirror installed in the wheelhouse is useful.

Overtaking

Many barge owners will spend their time in the relatively confined waters of canals. Barges overtaking too close and too fast can create the vacuum effect between them. As the faster overtaking barge draws the water away, the overtaken barge can then be pulled into the hole and, if too close, result in a collision with the stern as you are drawn inexorably in. If you are too close to the shore you can also be grounded by this effect

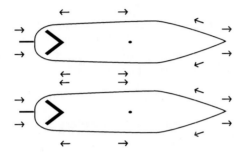

Passing

You may not be involved in much 'ships passing in the night' but passing an oncoming barge in confined channels such as canal or river can also produce a set of computations. Having considered how little water you have got beneath you, you might now realise how much less the oncoming, fully loaded, commercial barge hasn't got. Again the vacuum effect needs to be thought about. You also need to avoid being pushed too far over to the bank in your attempts to miss what looks like an inevitable collision. In this case the trick is to steer slightly

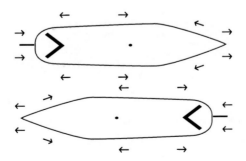

off the bow of the oncoming vessel and then proscribe a gentle sweep down the side. His bow wave will push you away but the following vacuum will draw you in. You may need to apply a burst of power to push your stern around and clear at the end. All of this, as ever, will be affected by the speeds of the closing vessels. If both vessels are travelling slowly enough then you can pass quite close. But don't go so slowly as to lose steerage way and don't go too close to the bank in order to give him space. You risk being swept ashore and he will continue happily on without so much as a backward glance. The other, slightly unnerving, situation occurs when the oncoming ship is running empty. His bow is very high out of the water and you can't see his wheelhouse. So you don't know whether he has seen you or not. Hopefully he will have a camera on the bow but this may not be so. Adjust your actions accordingly. Good luck.

TIP: Remember that in very shallow waters the pivot point moves slightly further aft

TIP: Convention requires that vessels travel 'on the right' passing each other port to port. In mainland Europe barges over 20m length must carry a visible Blue Flag / Board which must be displayed if you wish to pass on the wrong side. Although my barge is actually 19.8m I still carry a loose flag which can be used to acknowledge the signal from a barge displaying his board. (*See* CEVNI Rules)

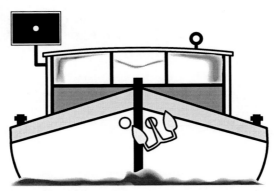

Barge showing the blue flag. This symbol appears on the cover of the magazine of DBA The Barge Association titled 'Blue Flag"

We encountered this push-tow in the Netherlands as we emerged from the River Lek and turned south into the Noord Canal. It had come from the Port of Rotterdam. You can get some idea of the scale by counting the number of cars parked on the aft roef* deck. What is not clear from the photo is that there is another, third, dumb barge on the starboard side equally loaded with containers. Handling a push-tow of this dimension takes some skill.

What is also not apparent is the fact that there was a 3500 tonne fully laden commercial barge coming up from the south approaching our port side. We swiftly moved over to port to allow him space and showed our Blue Flag to signify that we would pass on the wrong side.

We were on a 14-hour passage from Amsterdam to Willemstad on the Hollands Diep and very glad when we dropped the anchor outside the lock at Volkeraksluizen. The next morning, waiting on the pontoon at the lock, we discovered that the Dutch do not have an orderly queuing system especially on a holiday weekend. As someone remarked at the time, 'It is no good being English here!'

* This is the Dutch name for the aft cabin.

TOWING

Advanced Technique

This is an advanced technique, and is a skill in itself. It is recommended that you don't attempt it until you have gained experience Knowing how to do a Tugman's Hitch doesn't qualify. Hopefully you will never have to engage in towing. But engines, gearboxes and propellers being what they are, it may occur and I have towed and been towed. The following is included to give some idea of what is involved.

The length of tow rope will be determined by whether you are in confined waters or at sea. The rope needs to be seriously strong. Not one of your mooring lines. If at sea, you will need quite a long hawser and, to prevent it snatching, it helps if some serious weight such as a small anchor or length of chain is suspended somewhere near the middle. This will keep the line taut. The rope should be cradled on to the ends of each ship if possible to spread the load and keep you straight. You can also use the anchor and chain of the towed vessel with a warp carried on to the towing vessel. Don't forget to show the appropriate signals or lights.

On a river or canal you will manage with something much shorter. Ease forward very slowly to prevent the rope snatching. This will cause your barge to be jerked back and will pull you off course. Be prepared, with axe or quick release mechanism, to cast off the tow if needed. But keep your crew away from the lines since a snapping line under tension can whip round with devastating effect.

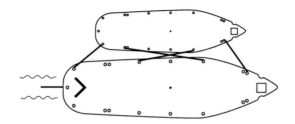

You can also tow by breasting up alongside. You will need a seriously good rope as a towing spring which will do most of the work. Lines at bow and stern will keep the vessels together and a forward spring should be deployed to prevent the tow surging ahead when you slow down or stop.

Remember that any dead weight on one side will drag the barge round. If you have to do a turn with a vessel alongside make sure that it is on the inside of the circle otherwise the drag of the dead weight won't allow you to get round. The stern of the towing vessel should be as far aft of the end of the tow as practical or you won't have steerage. You will notice, for example, that enormous commercial loads are moved by push-tows nowadays. This gives them control of the pivot point.

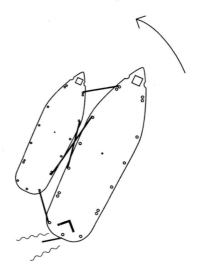

TIP: Towing a dinghy is not easy with a barge if you are passing through locks. They always get tangled up on the wrong side of the rudder and crushed against the wall when you go astern. Try to carry it onboard either on davits or on deck. If you do have to tow it then it may be best to have it on a short line pulled up tight to the stern. Whether it's tight or on a long line, adjust the length so that the dinghy planes on your wake wave. This will stop it ploughing into the water and thereby reduce the considerable drag factor.

DISCLAIMER

Remember that all barges are different and the circumstances in which they are being used will vary. The author cannot accept any responsibility howsoever caused for any actions or consequences which may occur as a result of reading this book, acting upon its contents or thinking you know what you are doing.

ANCHORING

Anchoring is something you will be taught at seamanship classes but here are some pertinent points for barges.

The first rule of anchoring is to make sure that you are in a designated or permitted area. Not only are there lots of places with underwater cables and pipes but also areas where you might cause an obstruction to the navigation. Remember, the barge owner is not permitted to drop anchor in most canals and some rivers. Puncturing the lining of the bed or blocking the navigation are not popular. The principal bow anchor(s) should be of a size commensurate to your barge. Take advice from your surveyor if you aren't sure. It isn't the weight of the anchor that really matters. Most of the work is done by the weight of the chain laid down on the bed. The rule of thumb is that you need an absolute minimum of three times as much chain laid onto the bottom as the maximum (including rising tide) depth of water. You can use more than this: the heavier the barge, the more you will need. It depends on the conditions in which you are anchoring – such as a muddy or rocky bottom or gale-force winds. There are different anchors for different ground but a stockless anchor is best for barges.

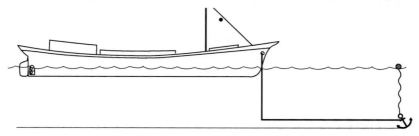

You will also need a kedge anchor positioned at the stern. This is a secondary and lighter anchor. On larger barges this will have its own winch but smaller barges can manage with something which can be lifted by hand. On my barge I also carry a heavy weight which can be secured to a warp or chain. This works as a mud anchor and won't hook into the ground.

With the main anchor laid, you need to ensure that it is holding properly. Reverse gently against it to make sure it isn't dragging. Once satisfied you should take compass bearings from two or more fixed objects on the land so you can monitor whether the barge is drifting.

Finally, and depending on where you are, you will need to show the appropriate signs. A round ball should be flown in the for'ard rigging. If you haven't got the real thing then a small tyre or even a frying pan will suffice. You may also be required to have a yellow marker buoy (CEVNI) attached to the anchor itself to show its position on the bed. If you are anchoring in confined spaces make sure that you have allowed enough space for the barge to swing round without hitting another vessel.

TIP: Once the anchor is laid, you should lock the chain either with the clamp on the winch or by shackling to a specified fitting secured to the ship. The winch should be re-set ready to weigh anchor. Once the anchor is up, the winch should be prepared for dropping again. Always be prepared for the next move.

TIP: Ensure that your anchor winch and chain are in good working order, greased and ready to be used instantly. On old working barges, where the anchor hasn't been used for some time, winches have often seized up. Make sure that any crew involved are completely au fait with the mechanism. You may need the anchor in a hurry and this isn't the time to start teaching. Ensure that there is no loose chain or warp which can catch on feet and pull you over. Keep fingers out of the winch. This is a common place for mishaps.

BUOYS

Picking up a mooring on a buoy from a barge requires a delicate touch. Approach the buoy from downwind/stream and come up to it on the upstream side so that the barge is pushed down onto it. Allow the buoy to come along the side of the barge until a crewman, with line already secured on the bow, can slip the loose end through the eye and bring it back to the bow. On very large ship buoys this may need two crew – one to position the line at the eye and the other to pull it through with a boathook. If you are staying for a while put a second safety line on the buoy in case one breaks.

I had occasion to do some repairs to my sterngear in tidal waters. I needed to bottom out on a falling tide so the barge lay alongside a causeway. First I set the main anchor uptide of the required destination. Then I took the kedge out in the dinghy to a position uptide of the stern. By playing out the two anchor chains I was able to position the barge beam on to the tide and alongside the underwater causeway.

Secure the rudder

On a berth which is subject to either strong current or tide running into your stern, you may need to lock or lash the rudder amidships. This will prevent the rudder being pushed round by the current. If it goes past the magic 35 degree angle it may be anything between hard and impossible to get it back to the centre again. Some steering wheels have a locking mechanism on the shaft behind the wheel. If not, then set up some light lines or cords which can be tied off to any adjacent fixture. Most important – don't forget to release it before you set off again.

Fouled Prop / Prop Wrap

Sooner or later your prop will get wrapped up with rope, wire, plastic or some other hidden detritus. First you notice an unexplained change in engine pitch. If it is a big wrap-up your engine will stall. In open waters you can probably drift for a bit while you get down there with a knife. You may have to consider dropping the anchor. If running downstream in a narrow waterway, use the aft anchor or you will swing across the navigation. Usually barge props, being close to the surface and well aft, aren't too difficult to reach. I can get to mine by leaning over the side of a dinghy. I also have a horizontal bar above the cavitation plate which supports a plank run out from the quayside. Alongside your razor sharp axe will be an equally sharp knife. Divers knives are good for this. But if you have a heavy wrap up, especially synthetic rope, you may need a hacksaw blade to get through it. A lifejacket should be worn plus a hard hat to prevent head damage in case you get banged against the hull. Preferably carry a strong and willing youth who can be despatched to do the job leaving you free to offer advice, sharpen the knife and drink tea.

TIP: fix a cord on to the tool you are using and loop it round your wrist. It isn't much good on the bottom.

TIP: another useful trick is to sharpen the hook and point on a boathook which can be deployed from the lockside to remove lighter ropes etc.

On one of my regular trips on the tidal Thames, I was running upstream with a good tide behind me. Deciding to stop at Chiswick, I passed the pier and rounded up to head into the rising tide. Engaging reverse gear to slow down and start the turn there was a horrible clunk and the engine stalled. There was something round the prop. Now being carried upstream beam on and powerless I decided to drop the anchor. The bottom of the river at this point is hard shingle and the anchor didn't hook in. With all the chain run out it was bouncing along the bottom at speed. Chiswick Railway Bridge was now uncomfortably close but finally the anchor got a bite in the softer ground on the inside of the bend. It took an hour in the water to cut the 2" nylon tug hawser off the propeller. Mercifully it was summer time.

SINGLE HANDED

Advanced Technique

Managing a barge single-handed is not as daunting as you might think. Once you have got used to your barge and how it handles, your heart won't beat quite so fast. The important thing is to get it set up properly. All ropes, fenders, poles and so forth should be positioned on both sides of the barge where needed And here we go again – do it slowly or even more slowly.

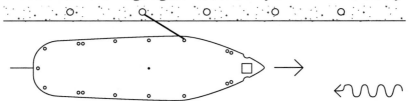

This will give you time to stroll nonchalantly up the side deck, pick up the line which you have set up at the midship bitts (cleats) and get an eye or a loop on to a suitable shore bollard. The line can then be taken a couple of times round the bitt and played out slowly to bring the ship to rest. By using a midships cleat you will end up with the barge laying alongside rather than being whipped away at one end as it swings. Barges rigged for sail may prove more difficult to manage alone since side decks are usually quite cluttered and the lee boards are inconveniently positioned smack in the middle. In an ideal world you will have come into the mooring so slowly as to be nearly at a dead stop before you leave the wheelhouse. Try and avoid using too much reverse gear if it makes your stern swing about too much. Another useful trick is to make up a big plunger vacuum flask of hot water, tea or coffee to keep in the wheelhouse so you don't need to keep diving down to the galley. Oh, and a handy pot to p........

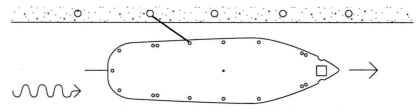

CAUTION: Wear a self inflating lifejacket. There may not be anyone to pull you out.
TIP: Practise working the barge single handed when you are not alone. You and your main crew should be equally capable.

Part Three

ROPE

Types of Ropes

Materials, Strength & Properties

Modern ropes are very much stronger for their size than the massive old natural hemps of yesteryear. If you choose rope that looks big enough for your huge barge then it is almost certainly bigger than you actually need. Remember you have to handle this stuff and smaller is easier. Ideally you will have several different types and sizes in your rope locker.

There are many types of rope and combinations of materials available to the modern boater. Here is a brief guide to some of the basic factors. Your final choice will depend on the size of your barge and the use you put it to.

Nylon has the advantage of stretching, which is good for mooring lines where surge is experienced and a bit of 'give' is useful. The disadvantage is that it sinks and could get fouled in your prop. It is the strongest but loses 10% to 20% of its strength when wet. It has very good UV resistance to sunlight but deteriorates if left out getting wet. Over time it also becomes rough to handle.

Polyester does float, but doesn't have the same shock factor. It is used for braided ropes, has the strongest weight ratio but is expensive. A natural buff version is available but costly.

Polyprop has a lower weight ratio, good UV characteristic, and doesn't sink. It is what 'Hardy Hemp' or hempex is made of and is a good economical all round rope for barges. It comes in a natural hemp colour, looks the part on old vessels, is easy to use and feels good.

There are many variations on construction of rope. Braided ropes are superior and lay down and store easily, but are very expensive. 3-strand laid rope is more economical but has to be coiled carefully in the right direction.

Sizes between 18mm and 24mm are the most commonly used depending on the purpose and the weight of your barge and your choice of rope. Extremely heavy barges may feel the need to go up to 36mm for selected purposes. Take advice from your rope supplier. Some navigation authorities set down specific criteria for weight ratio. Generally these are designed for commercial ships carrying full cargo. Unless you intend to ship a lot of wine they are unlikely to affect you.

CAUTION: Look after your ropes. They deteriorate over time. Your safety will depend on them.

TIP: Natural fibre rope needs to be stored dry. Artificial fibres are more water resistant but gradually degrade when left out in sunlight.

Rope Names

Sailing ships have a multitude of ropes and giving them specific names helps to identify them and their purpose. The terms most used on motor barges are confined to Rope, Line, Warp and Halyard. For example a spring line is a rope so they mean much the same thing. Warp, however, is the name given to a rope specifically designated as a main mooring rope and designed to pull a vessel into a mooring (warping). It can also be a towing rope and, in the absence of chain, an anchor rope. At the other end of the scale a halyard is a line specifically used to raise and lower sails and flags.

Nautical Terms

Belay	make fast a rope
Bend	form of knot which ties two rope ends together
Bight	any usable part of a rope (not the standing part or the ends)
Bitter end	loose inboard end of rope or warp (behind the bitts). inboard end of anchor chain.
Bowline	type of knot creating an eye in the end
Cast off	to let go the ropes, release the vessel
Check	ease rope slowly to stop vessel moving
Ease	allow rope to slacken under control
Eye	loop spliced into end of rope or formed by bowline
Halyard	rope for lifting sail or flag
Haul	pull
Hawser	heavy towing or mooring line (often wire rope)
Heaving line	light line with heavy weighted end
Hitch	method of securing rope to object other than rope
Lay	direction of twists in stranded (laid) rope
Make fast / off	secure a vessel, rope,
Painter	rope from bow of dinghy for towing
Snub	prevent (stop) rope from running out round bitts, cleats etc
Spring	line running fore or aft to another place (dockside or vessel)
Standing part	fixed part of rope which doesn't run (made off at each end)
Surge	controlled movement of rope round bitts / bollard / winch drum
Take a turn	wrap rope round bitts / bollard
Warps	rope for mooring, moving with rope, or anchoring
Warping	doing the above

Knots, Hitches and Splices

There are many good books and you will, unless you are sailing, use only a few in your daily life. Get a book which covers the basics and has clear illustrations. Basics include the bowline, the round turn with hitches, the rolling and the clove hitch. The tugman's hitch is ideal for making off big ropes onto large bollards and bitts (*see* **Bitts and Bollards**). I'll let other books show you how to splice.

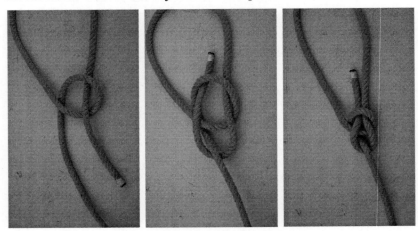

Three stages of the bowline

Mooring Ropes

These will be your biggest ropes and you need a minimum of six. Two need to be about 1.5 x the length of your barge which will be deployed as fore and aft springs (*see* **Securing**) The other four can be a little shorter to act as bow and stern lines. You should have head and stern lines running slightly fore

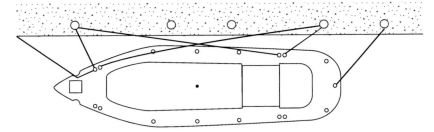

and aft of the barge to prevent the ends being swung away by any current. Breast lines will also be deployed at bow and stern which hold the ship into the side. If you are moored in tidal waters you may need longer lines to cope with extremes of rise and fall. When calculating the length it is worth allowing a bit extra. This permits remaking of a damaged spliced eye without losing the required length.

Handling Ropes

Ropes for working the ship through locks and for casual mooring can be both shorter and lighter. 15 – 20 metres should suffice and you may choose to have one at each corner of the barge. In some cases, perhaps on a smaller barge, one at each end will be fine. Always leave them lightly coiled on the deck so that they run out easily and don't snag. Coil them down in the direction of the lay of the rope (clockwise) so that they lie flat. You may need them in a hurry so don't wind them up too tight and don't tie them up either. This only needs to be done when they are being stored away. It is also very useful to have a couple of quite short lines of about five metres. These can be used in tight situations such as floating bollards in a lock chamber, if you are tied up alongside an adjoining vessel or if you want to hold the barge in tight so there isn't a big gap between you and the shore. But watch out for any possible variations in the water level to prevent being hung up or pulled down if the level changes.

Having a selection of shorter lines means that you don't clutter the decks, and risk a trip, by having miles of un-needed rope. It is worth while keeping a long length of older rope which you have taken out of service and replaced with new. This could be used in a situation where you may not be able to retrieve it and don't mind the loss. A heaving line is another useful addition to your locker. This requires a light line, perhaps braided nylon, with a very heavy weight on the end. The weight should be protected with some snazzy ropework to make it soft on impact. This line will carry much further than the heavier stuff and can be attached to the big one to be hauled out to the shore or back to the barge. You can make your own weight with a small canvas bag filled with sand.

Securing the Barge

Normal practice for securing a vessel is to have bow and stern lines running ashore with two springs, fore and aft, to prevent the barge surging backwards and forwards on the mooring. This is also vital where passing vessels will set up a surge.

Allowance should always be made for changes in the water level and to the possibility of unexpected variations as well. This could be caused by heavy rain bringing the level up or by something causing it to drop such as a canal bank breach. Obvious and predicted changes caused by tide, which can be very extreme, will mean that your springs need to be long enough to scissor you up or down. Bow and stern ropes should also accommodate the change. If you are on a new tidal berth you will need to stay with the ship while the change occurs. Assuming you are bow up to a falling tide then let the aft spring take the strain as the barge moves up (or down). Bow and stern can be slackened until you stop moving. Finally the fore spring can be adjusted and made off. Now you know that the barge will simply rise and fall on the lines. Remember that the weight of a heavy mooring line will pull the barge into the side. On my home mooring I use chain for the fore and aft lines with a short rope length attached to make off on to the barge. This is both strong and heavy.

When tied up where there is a big vertical difference in height you will notice that the fore and aft breast lines will not hold the barge in tight. You may need to run these lines further forward or aft, or even to the other side of your barge, to hold you in.

TIP: beware of changes in level which might cause you to get hung up or pulled down by vertical lines.

When mooring on your travels you can take a lighter approach to the use of lines. However the principles are the same. Make sure that your shore lines cannot be slipped off by the passing gentry. Never simply drop an eye over a bollard because it can easily be cast off. At minimum make sure that the eye is doubled round the bollard. A cable tie can be used to pinch the remaining parts of the open eye together thereby stopping it from being removed casually. Always make off the rope on the barge, perhaps on the side away from the bank. You may choose to make up some cunning device with chain at the shore end of the rope which can be padlocked or shackled to itself making it

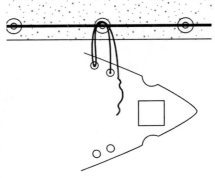

very difficult to remove. Remember, however, that you may need to cast off in a hurry so be prepared for this eventuality. If you are making off to either a ring or a post, and it isn't too far away, you can pass a long loop through the ring, return it to your bitts and then pull in the loose end and make it off. When casting off you can control the rope entirely from your deck by untying your end, slipping the loop off the bitts and then pulling it back through the ring. This means you don't have to pull the entire length of line back through the ring.

Always pass a line through a ring from underneath so that the free end comes over the top. This will prevent the rope jamming on the ring when you pull it back.

Wrong! This will trap the rope.

Correct, the rope can pull free.

If you can find them, or have them made, a couple of ground (land) anchors are also very useful especially in rural areas. These have a single fluke which is hooked firmly into the ground, and an eye or two on the top to secure the line. If you can't find any then you can make your own version from mild steel.

Another very ingenious trick is to use two mooring spikes with rings welded on the top. Drive them in at opposite angles, rather like an X shape, until the tops meet and it looks like an inverted V. Spliced eyes can be put over the spikes, the rings can then be padlocked or shackled together and the ropes run to the fore and aft ends of your barge to act as springs. If you use nylon rope you will get a bit of shock absorption built in. Since the spikes are going away at an angle into the ground this device and the ropes are almost impossible to remove unless you dig them out.

TIP: Additional security in places where there is a risk of being cast adrift can be had by dropping an anchor (or two) which will stop you being swept away.

TIP: Never pull the 'eyed' end of a rope round a bollard or through an eye or ring. Chances are it will get jammed or hooked up especially if it was formed with a bowline. Always pull the end which is not made up which should be whipped but not back spliced. You need it to run through without hindrance.

TIP: If you are leaving your barge unattended in an urban mooring you should look for ways to prevent it being cast off. Look for any possible places down the side of the wharf, wall or campshedding where you can shackle a chain to the wall. The

chain can be short but needs to be long enough to allow for any height variations. It may not hold the barge close to the bank but it will prevent you taking an unwanted trip over the weir.

TIP: If the spliced eye on your rope isn't big enough you can quickly make it bigger. Put your hand through the eye, and pull the bight through the eye. The resultant loop will now pull tight round a bollard. Conversely this works well if your eye is very big and you want to reduce it.

TIP: Keep a few super large 'big ship' shackles in your locker. Along with short lengths of chain they are useful when inventing tricks for mooring up.

TIP: A small grappling iron can be useful to hook on to trees.

Working the Barge with Rope

This is a huge subject so this book will focus on only some of the aspects that are relevant to barge handling. Working bargees used ropes extensively having developed the skills before engines were employed. I have mentioned earlier that the use of rope to manage the barge is important but often under used. It goes along with the 'go slow or even slower' philosophy and gives you good control of your barge since you are, essentially, still attached all the time. Here are just a few ideas to encourage you to think about using rope to carry out some manoeuvres.

One of the most useful is employed to get your barge around a tight corner without the aid of a bowthruster (opposite). This is simple – with the aid of a line. It is an example of combining rope and engine power. You may need to get a crewman ashore or enlist the help of a bystander. These are usually to be found, watching you carefully, whenever you attempt a difficult move. The principle is simple. Get a line ashore, or on to whatever it is you are trying to swing around. Perhaps by now your rope skills will be such that you can throw the eye onto a bollard (*see* p72). Make it fast to the bow or to the side cleat nearest your pivot point. Calculate the length to allow the bow to come round the corner. You'll need someone to standby on this rope to play it out or shorten it as the manoeuvre proceeds. Move the barge slowly forward and when the line goes tight turn the wheel to drive the stern round. The line will prevent you being swept onto the far side and you can swing, elegantly and without smashing into anything, around the corner. Watch your stern as you come round.

Using ropes is a secure way of extricating a barge from an inshore berth. First set up lines that can be used to pull the outside vessel back in to the shore. Others can be set up to pull the departing vessel out. Keep a line ashore at the aft end of the vessels. Run another line from the shore around the same end of the inside ship. This doesn't need to go right up to the bows since it can be moved for'ard on the outside vessel as the inside vessel moves out. Make sure it goes round everything including the flag pole. This loose line will now be used to pull the bow of the outside vessel back in to the bank. Even though the outside vessel isn't going anywhere the engine should be kept running. It may be needed to maintain position if there is any current running or if it has to cast off and leave the berth.

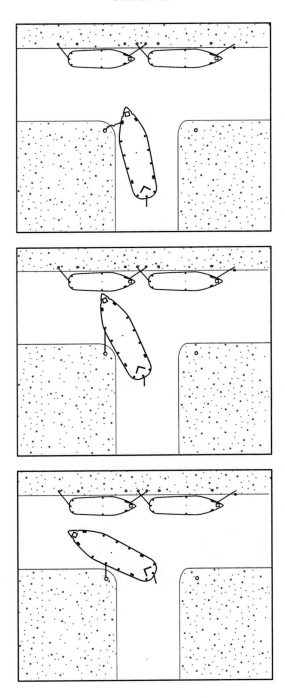

Throwing, Braking, Making off

Throwing an Eye

Horses for courses, people have different preferences in this matter. If you want to throw a spliced eye on to a bollard you will need three things. First: the right type of rope which shouldn't be so stiff or so soft as to make it difficult to throw. Second: the eye needs to be of a good size to open up and drop over the bollard. Third: you need to practise a lot, a lot, a lot......and believe you will succeed

Hold the eye open like a lasso with the hand gripping the beginning of the eye against the standing part. Prepare a calculated length of rope which will fly out to the bollard with the remainder loosely coiled on the deck. Keeping your eye on the target, throw the eye out round your side releasing the line with your hand pointing at the bollard. The loop should fly out at an angle so that the top goes over the bollard and the bottom catches on it. It will then drop onto the target.This technique is commonly used in Freycinet locks in France

 where you drop the eye over the bollard as you pass it and then take up the braking action on your for'ard bitt to ease the ship down. In big commercial locks you will be able simply to drop the eye onto a floating bollard set into the wall

TIP: Ensure that spliced eyes are not only big enough to go over bollards but will allow the eye to be removed from a distance. This involves flicking a ripple along the rope so that the eye jumps off the bollard.

Throwing a Loop

Keeping the eye secured on your bitts and throwing a loop of rope out over the bollard may work better for you or for the circumstances to hand. It is certainly easier for the novice rope thrower. Again you need rope of the correct flexibility and of adequate length. With the eye secured on your bitts prepare a rope which is long enough to reach the target and return to the deck with some to spare. Coil enough in the left hand to go past the bollard, allow a space and then coil a similar amount in the right hand. Holding the left hand away from your body throw the right hand out towards the right side of the bollard. As the rope flies out release the coil in the left hand. This should send a suitable amount of rope out towards both sides of the target. Alternatively you can throw both coils at once. Make sure there is enough rope left on board to haul in or you will have a loose line draped over the lockside. The common difficulty with this technique is not throwing enough rope out to reach the target. It is not a problem if you throw an excess length so long as it drops around the bollard. It can then be brought in tight and made off on your bitts. Be careful not to cross the line over when it returns to the barge. The most important thing is that you are comfortable and effective with your chosen technique. Your helmsman will be forever in your debt.

Wrong!   Correct

TIP: Deck crew should give a clear signal to the helmsman when the rope has been successfully secured

TIP: When slowing the barge to a halt by easing the rope around the bitt, make sure that you don't make it off until the barge has stopped. This prevents the barge being stopped abruptly which causes the aft end to swing out and upsets the helmsman.

Making Off

With your line safely attached to the shore-side, the next thing is to slow the barge and make off at your end. This is where these massive bitts are important. By taking one turn round the bottom of the bitt you apply friction to the rope and start slowing the ship down. As it slows take another turn above the first pin which separates the rope and slows it further. The third turn will brake it to a standstill. The fourth, final, turn will lock the rope around the bitt. Now you can make it off.

Tugman's Hitch

This is also known as a Bargeman's Hitch. The best method of making off the rope for big barges and big bitts is the tugman's hitch. Its name alone implies serious seamanship at work. It simply requires a loop of rope to be passed round the taut line (standing part) and dropped over the top of the bitt. It is easily undone by flipping the loop off the top of the bitt even when the line is taut. Another turn round the bitt in the opposite direction secures the hitch. If you are staying for a while you can apply a second tugman's in the opposite direction to the first making it very secure. If your stop is going to be brief you can substitute the tugman's with a half hitch on to the top of the bitt. This is useful if you need to make the bow fast quickly to allow the helmsman to drive the barge forward against the line. When you are stopped in the right position you can substitute it for the tugman's if preferred.

TIP: Always work the ropes in a standing position with enough rope in hand to swing it round the bitt. Don't get down on your knees because you can't react so quickly to an emergency. You may need to get out of the way fast. Keep hands well away from the bitts until the barge has stopped. Many a finger has been trapped and crushed between rope and a hard place.

TIP: Make sure you use hitches which can be easily undone even when the rope is under strain.

TIP: When putting your eye onto a bollard which already has one from another vessel, pass your eye up through the inside of the eye on the bollard and then drop it over the top. This will permit the first eye to be removed without being trapped by yours and you can still remove yours if you leave first.

CAUTION!: Keep your feet clear of rope on the deck. Don't stand on it and don't stand in a loop. Many an accident has been caused by rope flying out and taking the crewman with it.

TIP: Always work the ropes from onboard. Do not jump off with a rope and expect to stop the barge. You aren't strong enough, you don't have control and you are more useful on board.

TIP: When working with stranded rope always run it round the bitts in the same direction (usually clockwise) as the lay of the rope. This will prevent kinking and make it easier to use.

Useful Tools

Some locks can be very deep and options to throw up a line almost out of the question, especially if you have a small low barge. You may, but probably may not, get help from the lockkeeper. A useful tool in this situation is to have a pole with a stiff wire loop at the end. The eye of your line can be held on this, you reach up the lock side and, bingo, drop the line over the bollard. Magic.

WARPING

Moving a barge with ropes alone far preceeds any use of engines. Known as warping, this remains a simple and sensible way of moving the barge around a dock or moving it from one berth to another. It avoids all the stress of attempting manoeuvres using only the engine which can create more aggravation than the simple use of warps. It may take a little time to set up the ropes and the movement will be slow and peaceful. Remember that a heavy rope, especially when wet, will move a barge by its weight alone. Warping should not involve huge effort. Once the barge has started to move it will drift slowly along on its own momentum. You will need to set up lines which not only keep the barge in place but will also act as a brake line when you arrive at the destined spot. If you can find a suitable bollard or bitt take a turn round it and either pull, or stand, on the taut rope. When it has gone slack because the ship is moving again take up the turn on the bollard and repeat. Equally the ship can be slowed and stopped by taking a turn or two around a bollard and gradually applying braking tension. The tranquillity of this kind of manoeuvring allows a quiet time to exchange tales of horrendous experiences.

If you are hauling the barge along a canal the tow rope should be attached to the ship as close to the pivot point as possible. If it is attached at the bow it will simply pull the barge into the bank and too far aft will pull the bow away. You will still need to steer.

PART FOUR

Equipment

Part Four looks at some of the ancilliary aspects affecting or relating to the movement, equipment and management of a barge.

Steering Position

The position the helmsman occupies on the barge will have a major impact on how easy the barge is to handle. Ideally you should be able to see all four 'corners' just by turning round. Euro rules apply specific design criteria to new-build barges for this purpose. However old barges don't always offer that degree of comfort. Side doors on the wheelhouse make managing the barge both easier and safer.

Tiller Steering

You won't find many motor barges with tiller steering these days. The high thrust from the propeller makes it very hard to steer without mechanical aids such as blocks and tackle. Sailing barges will have either tiller or wheel depending on type and size. Handling a barge under sail is not the subject of this book. However, motoring a sailing barge is the same as handling a motor barge.

Wheel Steering

Your contact with your barge is, of course, primarily through your hands on the wheel. It is also through your feet and sensing how the barge is moving will be transmitted through both. Whether you have direct mechanical steering connections or a hydraulic system you will soon learn how to feel and interpret the information coming back to you.

Direct mechanical connection between wheel and rudder can be either by means of a solid shaft and cam system or by a mixture of chain or wire connected to a quadrant on the rudder post. This often allows the rudder to be turned round through 90 degrees flat against the transom. However many rudders will be fitted with stop chains from the rudder to the hull preventing the rudder from going round too far. If this happens with a strong current behind you it is almost impossible to get a long rudder blade back in line again so a limiting device is sensible. It can always be disabled if you need to fold the rudder flat. On a chain and wire system there should be minimum possible slack or you will get a sloppy response between wheel and rudder blade. However be careful not to overtighten or the system will 'seize'. You need a little play to provide a shock-absorbing effect especially with long rudder blades.

Hydraulic systems offer a considerable mechanical advantage giving you power steering. However they will rarely turn past the 35-degree arc due to the limitations of the ram length. A few barge owners have managed to come up with techniques to extend this. Hydraulic systems need to be installed to a very high standard because if they fail, which has been known, then you may have considerable difficulty resolving the problem. They need specialist skills and equipment to repair.

Gearing of the steering will depend on the system involved. The number of reduction gears, the size of the quadrant and how big the wheel is all play a part in this calculation. Ideally you want to achieve a balance which gives a good response when the wheel is moved. Too few turns will be very heavy and too many will be too light. Both of these are very tiring. Generally speaking, getting it geared to between 4 and 8 complete turns from lock to lock provides effective and comfortable control.

Rudder Position Indicator

Having a mechanical device situated before the wheel and driven either directly from the shaft or electronically is a vital aid to handling the barge. If these are not present, or impossible to install, then you'll need to set up some kind of visual aid attached to the top of the rudder post. For many years I have relied on looking over my shoulder. The ensign staff is attached to the top of the emergency tiller housing so I can quickly see the angle of the rudder and what is behind me.

Emergency Steering

Losing the steering is not a comfortable experience. It can happen and an emergency rig is vital. Ideally this should be as simple as slotting a tiller bar into the top of the rudder post. Invariably loss of steering will occur where you have little space to manoeuvre so it is vital that the jury rig (*see* **Glossary**) can be set up in seconds. It is worth taking time to practise this with your crew. You may need to disable, or detach, the existing system to allow the rudder to operate freely.

Rudder Types

Sailing Barge Rudder A very long blade in the water of around 1m to 1.5m allows good steerage without engine power. When under power half of the prop thrust will pass by with little effect when the rudder is put over. If you use your barge for sailing you will need to keep the longer blade.

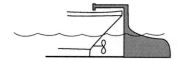 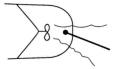

Balanced Rudders These have an extension to the blade which comes forward of the rudder post. When the rudder is turned there is an additional area of blade to take the thrust of the prop on both sides. Three quarters of the prop thrust will be diverted by the blade. This is a good improvement to fit if you can but may not be possible due to rudder post / propeller configuration.

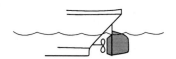 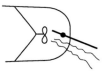

Twin Rudders Usually found on the larger commercial vessels twin rudders have very short blades and will deflect most of the prop wash. They are necessary if you have twin engines, which is rare, and they usually turn round to 90 degrees which is useful in small locks and when tied up at the quay.

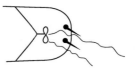

Rudder Blade Profiles. A simple improvement to water flow past the blade is to add a length of round bar or tube onto the trailing edge. Another is the Schilling rudder which is fish-shaped in section. Both of these improve the hydrodynamic flow round the blade

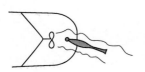

Rudder Improvements. The Becker rudder is highly regarded by those who have it. The design allows for the rudder to hinge vertically half way along its length. As it turns it pulls the end round rather like crooking your finger. This creates a scoop effect thereby directing the thrust even further round instead of just washing away behind. It takes the useful value past the 35-degree point and improves the hydrodynamics.

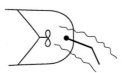

Some rudders have been fitted with a box designed in such a way as to turn a single rudder into a three-blade affair which improves the value of the thrust. This is useful when it isn't possible to fit a balanced blade.

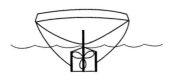

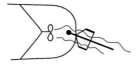

Anti-Cavitation Plates.

The propellers on unladen barges are only just below the surface and this can create a cavitation effect when under power. This is because the spinning prop creates a sort of whirlpool which pulls air down into a void. With less water around the propeller the power output is reduced. Anti-cavitation plates between prop and surface will cut out, or reduce, this effect. Often they are slightly curved or arched around the prop. The shape of your plates will affect the amount of prop walk. A propeller completely enclosed by a shield will reduce prop walk but it is difficult to remove stray rope, wire and debris if you get a fouled prop ('wrap up').

Size and Type of Propeller

This is the infamous 'Black Art' department. There are a number of computer programmes which claim to calculate the ideal size and shape of prop for your barge. The shape of prop you have will affect the handling characteristics. You may pick up speed quickly, stop dead or just thrash about without effect. Having the wrong type or size of prop, being sited too close to the stern post and subject to poor water flow from the hull will have a marked effect. You will soon learn the nature of yours and how to work with it or whether you should consider changing it.

Bow Thrusters

Principles

Most bow thrusters are simply a tube running transversly across the bow with a propeller inside.

A bow thruster is sometimes claimed to be an essential part of the machinery. Or it is described variously as useless, overstated, waste of space, dangerous and so on. They certainly have the ability to fail when most needed. It is vital that any bargee should know how to handle their barge without the use of this aid. Having done so you may wonder whether you need a bow thruster at all. The size and type of barge may affect your decision in this matter. The longer the barge and the higher the bow, the more useful one is. If it is going to be there then it must be big enough to do the job. It is not a cheap addition to a barge. There is one use which is not disputed. A bow thruster makes it easy to steer in a straight line when going astern by counteracting the paddle wheel effect on your pivot point. Incidentally, I think of the prop walk on my barge as a one-way bowthruster at the wrong end since it will push the bow over to starboard.

Drive Types

Bow thrusters may be driven by a dedicated engine, hydraulics or an electric motor. The last one is the most dangerous since it will only work while there is battery power. Prolonged use will flatten the battery very quickly which then has to be recharged, leaving you powerless meanwhile. The motors are also prone to burn out, rendering it useless. Another type is a rotating nozzle thruster set in a flat dish under the bow. This can be aimed in any desired direction and can be a seriously useful tool capable of propelling the barge, albeit slowly, entirely on its own. However they do protrude beneath your otherwise flat bottom so be careful taking to the ground and going into dock.

Fenders

There are many varieties of fender. Tyres are commonly used but are now frowned on in mainland Europe since they have the habit of breaking off and then sinking. Usually this happens in a lock where they can foul up behind the gates causing much grief all round. Zigzag fenders are now easily available and ideal for the job. The design incorporates a small amount of 'give' when compressed without bouncing the

barge off the wall. In the past, shippers used to make their own soft wood versions in the same shape which is tapered at each end and which can be smashed and replaced with ease. Like the modern zigzags, they have the advantage of floating when they fall off. Many bargees find that fenders are simply a nuisance when entering locks. They always seem to snag on something on the way in or out and don't use them. Inflated balloon fenders have the disadvantage of acting like bouncy balls so that when the barge hits the side it simply cannons off again thereby destroying your careful approach to lay alongside. Balloon fenders are fine to keep vessels apart when you are made fast and will cushion any blows. They should be used on a busy seaway where moored ships are thrown about by passing wash and will stop them grinding together. They are also useful if you are about to have a collision and a bit of cushion would be helpful. You may, of course, burst it in the process but it will soften the blow. Fender makers can also supply a variety of short, slim fenders which hang down the side, take up little space and will roll along the barge side which works well in locks. The other ideal fender material is rope. Big old, rotten ropes which are out of service can be fashioned into suitable shapes giving hours of harmless fun. They offer an ideal amount of give when hit and don't mark the paintwork.

(Well, you try taking a photo of a black fender against a black hull)

HOT TIP: Zigzag fenders can be cut in half allowing short ends to be hung down vertically. They can also be mounted horizontally, one above another, giving high and low protection and doubling as a boarding ladder.

CAUTION: People should not be used as fenders.

Bow Rudder

Before the introduction of bow thrusters, many of the larger commercial motor barges were fitted with retractable bow rudders. These were operated from the foredeck through a rudder box into which they could be withdrawn when not in use. There aren't many around and I've only seen one – which the owner never uses anyway. They may be useful if you have to do a lot of reversing or steer round a sharp bend but it needs another (bow) helmsman. Depending on the design it may either increase your draught or be an added hazard at the fore end especially if it hits the bottom. It may get bent and be impossible to draw up thereby compounding your problem.

Barge Poles & Boat Hooks

You will need a selection of boat hooks and poles. A short, lightweight, extending pole kept at each end of the barge is useful for picking up a line from the shore or on a mooring buoy. They aren't good for fending off the weight of a barge so you may choose to add a short but very stout pole for this purpose since long poles tend to swing about the ship and be quite hard to handle. A large U or V-shaped end on a pole allows you to hook this up to a bollard, railing or the bank which will keep it in place. This can be deployed as a fixed fend-off to hold the barge away from the bank. Longer poles are essential for pushing the ship away from the bank or poling off the bed of the waterway. Having two long poles, one of which has a hooked end and one without, should satisfy your needs. You can mark the pole with metre and half metre marks making it useful as a depth measure. On heavy commercial waterways this will not, in itself, suffice to control the barge but it might help. You can also invent serious metal pipe fend-offs if you are operating in waterways with sloping banks or other reasons which make it tricky to lay alongside the bank.

Remember that a human being is the weak link in the business of moving barges. You can move a barge more readily with the use of the engine or warps.

CAUTION: Keep hands and feet inboard. They are easily crushed.

Spud Legs

These are a very simple and effective idea. A tube is mounted, usually in the bow / fo'castle area, which goes straight down through the bottom of the hull. A leg or heavy tube is mounted into this which can be dropped down on to the river bankside or canal bed. This only works where there is a relatively low depth. The leg then 'spikes' the bow to the ground. It is excellent for holding the barge in position and keeping it from being swept on or off the bank. It needs to be both long and strong enough to resist bending from the sideways movement of the barge. A simple hand winch mechanism will pull the leg back up the tube. They can, of course, be fitted at each end of the barge if space permits but finding a convenient mounting space at the aft end may mean an unwanted intrusion into the aft cabin and machinery areas. Care should be taken where they are used. They would, for example, damage the bed of canals in the UK. Many would suggest that a spud leg is a more useful piece of equipment than a bow thruster – but it does a completely different job.

Leeboards

Often referred to as 'those flappy wings' leeboards are an important part of any flat bottomed sailing barge whether it be a Thames barge, a Humber Keel or a Dutch barge. Without them the boat will simply slip sideways when sailing. Authentically they were made with an aerofoil cross-section acting like a wing and pushing the vessel to windward. As the sailing barges converted to engine power, many skippers kept the leeboards to help them manoeuvre. When the original wooden ones needed replacing, much smaller, thinner boards, made of steel, were fitted: they were much easier to handle and maintain. Some motor barges still carry them and they can be useful to help in turning the barge or preventing sideslip or drift. If you want to fit them to a motor barge then relatively small steel ones will suffice but they increase your beam, get in the way in locks and when laying alongside.

Bilge Keels

Principle & Design

Bilge keels offer an alternative to leeboards. The idea is to fit a length of steel plate at right angles to the hull. Running fore and aft, they are placed at the turn of the bilge. The plates should not stick out past the flat side or the flat bottom of the hull. They might be around one quarter to a third of the length of the ship and mounted in the centre section on the straightest part of the hull.

Bilge Keel

They are vulnerable when the barge is in a canal or lock which has sloping sides and care should be taken not to get hung up on them. They may be welded on in such a way that any serious force from beneath will snap them off rather than cause damage to the hull itself. They can also be welded onto a flat plate of about 100mm width which is welded to the hull with the keel welded on to it. This will spread the load and avoid unwanted damage to the hull plates if damage occurs. Or you can weld angle iron on to the hull bolting the keel to it.

Care should be taken to ensure that they are running true along the hull to prevent any possible and unwanted rudder effect. The barge should be ballasted correctly with the stern only slightly deeper than the bow. Bilge keels which are too high or low at the front will act like planes giving too much lift or dip respectively to the front of the barge when travelling at speed.

Bilge Keels vs. Leeboards

Bilge keels do two useful things. They help to reduce roll when out on exposed waters and subjected to a beam sea. They also reduce sideslip and therefore help the way in which the barge turns. They have, essentially, the same effect as leeboards without getting in the way and they are in position and always working for you. In pure terms they are not as efficient as lee boards because they don't go as deep into the water. Bilge keels will also add drag to the ship at all times since they can't be lifted like leeboards. However you may consider their value to barge handling to be worth it. In spite of an earlier suggestion that 'a barge is not on rails' people who have fitted bilge keels tell you that they have that effect.

Steadying Sail.

Motor barges roll notoriously at sea and bilge keels will help to reduce this roll. A bilge keel of around 6m x 0.25m on each side offers an area of around 3 square metres under the water. Add a small steadying sail and the rolling will be less noticeable. This is only effective when the wind and sea are on your beam and you should allow for a little more leeway when plotting your course.

Flags & Wind Indicators

The wind being one of the three key forces at work, it is vital to know where it is coming from and how hard it is blowing. Your ensign fluttering at the stern provides one clue and you may have other burgees flying from rigging on the mast, even if it is only a short navigation mast. A strip of light cotton tied on a halyard also helps. Any pilot flag flown at the stemhead will also show you what is happening for'ard. For example, if you are coming out of a side canal or dock it will tell you what wind, direction and strength might be blowing across your bow as you emerge. When travelling at speed the flags will be blown back making the wind direction 'appear' to be further forward than it actually is.

Part Five

And Finally

This part looks at the people on board and what they need to know and do to make barge handling a safe and pleasurable experience.

DON'T PANIC

Icy calm is the name of the game. Whatever happens remember that you are in command and your reactions will affect the behaviour and ability of your crew. Most of the time your knowledge and skill will get you out of trouble. When it is completely beyond your control then ensure that nobody does anything heroic or stupid. Keep your crew safe and let the ship take the knock. You can always repair the barge but damaging a bargee is not a good idea. If you are involved in a beam-on collision get the crew to lie flat on the deck close to the coachroof sides. This is one of the strongest parts of the ship and may offer some protection. They shouldn't attempt to fend off with limbs or anything else and climbing on to the roof may expose them to flying debris.

Part Five

THE CREW

Training

This sounds a bit formal for leisure barging but your crew need to know what is going on and what to do. Clear instruction on what you, the skipper, require of them and what they can expect from you makes for relaxed and happy barging. Well, it's a whole lot better than shouting at each other so it is worth spending time on this. Good communications lead to good relationships and therefore a safer environment on board. With the barge set up with all the right ropes, fenders and so forth in all the right places you can give clear instructions on what you expect of the crew and how to do it. Techniques for getting lines on in the lock, using the right fender to protect the barge without bouncing it are basic requirements. If you have visitors joining your cruise it might be worth putting together a simple document which can be given on arrival. It can set out the dos and don'ts, safety stuff, how to use the loo or whatever else you think will help. Clarity before the event is better than a 'but I thought...' afterwards.

CAUTION: No running on deck. It is too easy to trip, especially for children.

It is interesting to note that, on commercial barges, it is often the woman to be found at the wheel. This leaves the heavier deck work to the man. Since you'll spend most of your time working the barge as a couple you should, in the interest of safety, be interchangable and equally skilled. Many teams find that it is often the woman who is the better helmsman. Something to do with...

Communications

All crew should follow the skipper's instruction unless they have very, very good reason not to. Equally, everyone should be prepared for any change of plan that develops during the course of a manoeuvre. This may happen because the skipper is unaware of a problem he can't see or he has to adapt his plan to suit changing circumstances. Keep an eye on the skipper for any instructions and be prepared to react swiftly.

There are two ways of communicating with your foredeck crew. Since you are probably warmly ensconced in a nice dry wheelhouse with your hands firmly on the wheel it is unlikely that you can simply shout to each other. Establishing a system of hand signals works fine. But you must work out signals which are simple, clear and unambiguous. You will have told them what your plan is before they go to the foredeck. Your system should include signals for getting a line ashore, slowly braking the barge round the bitt, making it off tight and releasing when you are ready to cast off.

Equally you may need the crew to give you signals regarding how close you are to something and whether to advance, stop or reverse.

Many bargees will invest in some form of electronic communication. A tannoy mounted on the wheelhouse will get the message for'ard but will also broadcast to all and sundry. A more subtle version has a loudspeaker mounted on the foredeck which the crew can speak into giving two-way dialogue. Well, bystanders can hear what the skipper thinks of the crew but not vice versa. Perhaps the ultimate version is the use of two-way radios which clip on to your jacket, keeping your hands free. These can be acquired quite cheaply and offer complete privacy so you can make your mistakes without broadcasting them. A good one will have a selection of channels.* A particular channel might be affected by other telecoms activity in the area – which will either jam the signal or give you some very odd instructions. You can then select the channel with the best signal instead of talking to the local taxi service.

As one skipper observed :'We are rarely on the same channel!'

SAFETY

Emergency Procedures

Assuming that your principal crew is your other half they should be as capable as you if an emergency arises. They should know how to drop the anchor, stop the engine and make emergency calls on the VHF radio. All crew should know the location of fire extinguishers and how to use them. Gas cut-off taps should be identified. They should also know where lifejackets are stored if they aren't already wearing them. Other life-saving equipment such as life rings, raft and a dinghy capable of being launched quickly should be explained. You should have basic life-saving skills such as resuscitation. In mainland Europe, very specific criteria are laid down for safety equipment depending on the size and use of the vessel.

Man Overboard

You will, of course, have learnt all about this in your seamanship classes.

It goes without saying that all crew working on deck should be equipped with lifejackets, particularly at sea or in busy commercial waterways. They should be self-inflating in case of an unconscious crewman. It is all too easy to be working on deck, lose your balance and hit your head on the way over the side. Keep life rings easily accessible just aft of the wheelhouse. This means they can be thrown quickly, from either side, if somebody goes into the water. Mine are not fitted with a line because Murphy's Law says that, however carefully your line is coiled, it will snag when thrown. This will result in your towing the life-ring further away from the person in the water. If you can get the ring close to them, without hitting them on the head, then you will have time to turn the ship and go back and pick them up without panic. At night, also throw an automatic light marker. Keep your eye on the casualty at all times. Approach from down stream/wind so you have more control of the barge. It is worth taking time to practise this manoeuvre with your regular crew since it could be either of you getting wet. Practise this with a fender, life-ring or unwanted relative. The barge should be equipped with suitable means of getting back on board. Boarding ladders should extend well down into the water so that you can get your foot on to the bottom rung. Another method, if you have a suitable rudder, is to fix ladder rungs or steps onto the sides. (This is also useful if you have to go and inspect the propeller.)

Unconscious Casualty

You should be prepared for an unconscious casualty. If you have some sort of a mast it should be possible to set it up with a boom which can swing outboard and from which a sling can be lowered. The casualty can then be manoeuvred into position and winched aboard. Failing this you will need to work out some system that you can manage. Just remember that an unconscious and very wet person weighs an awful lot. Using an inflatable dinghy is a good way of getting someone out of the water.

Guard Rails & Hand Holds

Barges of the size and type we have been discussing were designed and intended for inland waterways. In this respect they were not fitted with handrails or stanchions. Many conversions for leisure use will have some kind of grab rails running along the top sides of the coachroof. It may only be a raised edge to the roof which prevents rainwater running down the sides. Designated rails offer more security for the hand to grip. They are useful for lashing down loose equipment on the coachroof. Fenders can be hung from them but the cords will obstruct the side deck.

It is also advisable to have some form of handle on the sides of the wheelhouse or other high-sided structure. Remember that barges can roll a lot so having something to hold on to will help to stop you going over the side.

If you are using your barge out on open waters and at sea, then stanchions offer much more security for the leisure boater. It is comforting to have them if you are likely to have children on board and they permit you to position fenders easily. They should not, however, run across the top of your bitts. This will make handling ropes extremely difficult and potentially dangerous for that reason. If you have stanchions fitted, make sure they are not so low as to trip you up and over the side. Preferably keep them at, or above, knee height. The bad news with stanchions is that they are on the very sides of the barge and prone to damage. They will be the first to suffer if you have any collisions or are tied up alongside a high wall or other ship. This is the time for those nice fat balloon fenders. If possible make your stanchions removeable.

HOT TIPS:

**Be prepared for emergencies
Work out, and practise,
routines for such things as:**
– Unconscious skipper
– Stopped engine
– Dropping anchor
– Using VHF
– Man overboard
– Fire
– Isolating gas
– Operating bilge pumps
– Unblocking loos

Trainee crew

QUALIFICATIONS

A simple rule of thumb is that you must hold the qualifications or licences required by the country in which the vessel is registered.

At the time of writing, the UK doesn't require legal formal qualifications for operating a pleasure boat under 24m in length. However, managed under the auspices of the RYA (Royal Yacting Association), many courses and qualifications are available on a voluntary basis for differing types of craft and usage. Minimum requirements, through the RYA, which an English skipper should have are: Day Skipper and ICC CEVNI. (ICC is International Certificate of Competence – CEVNI is the Eurowaterways system of navigation rules and signs). The former will give you essential instruction in seamanship and basic navigation and the latter will be required if you are cruising anywhere outside the UK. Both will give you added confidence in the management and sailing of your barge. Obviously you can aspire to higher levels such as Yachtmaster which qualifies the holder for coastal and cross-Channel passages. It is unlikely you'll need Yachtmaster Ocean unless you have a seagoing vessel and plan to cross the Atlantic.

Qualifications for skippers operating outside the UK vary from territory to territory and are subject to review and change. The Netherlands, France, Belgium and Germany require skippers to hold specific licences by law. Much depends on where you intend to cruise, your barge size and if you are staying there for any length of time or just passing through. It is also more complicated if you are from the USA. Organisations such as DBA The Barge Association offer advice and updates on what is required for different sized barges. Qualifications usually cover vessels up to 24m but above this length they become more complicated. However barges of less than 15m are generally subject to less rigorous rules. No doubt the qualifications for driving large barges will become more stringent as time goes by. But whatever happens, the more qualifications and experience you have under your belt, the more confident you will feel.

It is worth noting that the Master or skipper who carries the qualifications, including radio operation, must be on board when under way even though the ship may be steered by an unqualified helmsman. The Master is ultimately responsible.

LITERATURE

DBA The Barge Association has an extensive and very useful 'shop' offering members a selection of manuals, videos, charts and books. These are also available through their website www.barges.org. It is worth noting that you will be required to carry, in the wheelhouse, a copy of the regulations issued by the waterways authorities for the country in which you are travelling. They are, of course, in Dutch, French or whatever, but you must carry them.

Barge Handling Instruction

Various courses are available in the Netherlands and France but you might need to brush up on your languages. In the UK the DBA can lead you to qualified instructors and examiners. You can, for example, take the RYA Day Skipper course and then add the ICC/CEVNI under the auspices of an approved examiner. Whatever courses you take, get as much hands-on instruction, practice and experience as you can.

DBA The Barge Association

The Association, started in 1992, brings together people interested in barges and barging. It is a voluntary company run by its members. It publishes six issues of a 40-page colour magazine each year and has a very useful bookshop aimed at the barge owner. The active website can be seen at www.barges.org and there are useful internet groups for discussion and advice. Membership, which can be applied for through the website, includes people from all over the world and is open to all. The DBA's modest annual subscription provides a wealth of knowledge and experience for its members. If you are serious about barging, it is a valuable resource.

ASSOCIATED BOOKS AND SOURCES OF INFORMATION
DBA The Barge Association – bookshop – www.barges.org
RYA Royal Yacting Association www.rya.org
Reed MacMillan Nautical Almanac

GLOSSARY

Abaft	behind
Abeam	on the beam, beside the vessel
Aboard	on board
Adrift	loose, untied
Aft	near the stern
Ahead	direction of travel, in front
Alongside	next to and touching vessel or berth
Amidships	rudder on centre course, middle of a vessel
Astern, go	travel backwards, behind
Athwart	across
Author	person talking out of his transom
Aweigh	anchor comes clear of the sea bed
Ballast	weight added to vessel to lower centre of gravity
Barge	flat bottomed freight boat for canals & rivers
Bargee	bargeman
Beam	width of vessel
Beam on	going sideways
Bearing	compass direction to or from another position
Belay	make fast a rope
Bend	form of knot which ties two ends together
Berth	place for vessel to dock; a bunk
Bight	any usable part of a rope (not standing part or the ends)
Bilge	curved side on bottom of vessel; underfloor area
Bitts	paired vertical posts for securing to
Bitter end	inboard end of rope or warp (behind the bitts) which is loose / inboard end of anchor chain
Blue Flag	blue board to indicate vessels passing each other on wrong side (CEVNI)
Boat	small vessel without decks propelled by oars

	or sails
Bollard	single vertical post for securing to
Bottom	all of the vessel below the waterline
Bottom out	aground, high & dry, bottom out of the water
Bowline	type of knot creating eye in ropes end
Bow	front of vessel
Breasting	side by side
Bridge Hole	navigable space under arch / span of bridge
Bulkhead	nautical brick wall, good for banging head
Bullnose	nose of brickwork at entrance to lock
Buoy	floating marker or mooring position: navigation mark
Burgee	triangular club flag
Campshed	steel sheets driven down creating / protecting bankside
Cast off	to let go
Check	ease rope slowly to stop vessel moving
Chine	angle between bottom and side plates underwater
Cleat	a fitting with projecting ears to tie onto
Coachroof	structure raised above deck level for accommodation
Coamings	raised sides surrounding cargo hatches to keep water out
Counter	area of stern overhanging the water
Course	direction ship is intending to go / is going
Craft	boat or vessel
Davits	small crane(s) to carry dinghy
Displacement	weight of vessel = water displaced
Draught	depth of vessel below water
Drive train	combination of engine, gearbox, shaft and propeller
Dock	berth for vessel; box in court for prosecuted mariners

Downstream	direction of current towards river mouth
Dumb barge	barge without power
Ebb	falling, outgoing tide
Ensign staff	flagpole on the aft end for national maritime flag only
Eye	loop in end of rope
Fairlead	fitting or hole on ship's side for running mooring line through
Fairway	usable channel
Fender	protection for side of vessel
Fend off	push or hold away
Flood	rising, incoming tide
Fore and Aft	centre line of ship
Forward	in the direction of the bow
G & T	drink made with juniper berries (G) & containing quinine (T) (lemon prevents scurvy)
Grappling iron	small 4-hooked anchor for throwing
Gunwales	sides of the hull above deck level
Halyard	rope for lifting sail or flag
Hard over	(to port or starboard) put wheel over to maximum useful or useable angle
Haul	pull
Hawser	heavy towing or mooring line (often wire rope)
Head	front of vessel
Heading	direction vessel is pointing
Heave to	stop or slow down head up to the wind
Heaving line	light line with heavy weighted end
Helm	wheel or tiller
Helmsman	person steering the vessel
Hitch	method of securing a rope to an object other than rope
Hull	all of the ship up to deck level

|---|---|

Glossary

Inboard	in to the ship
Jack staff	flagpole on the bow
Jury rig	emergency repair to solve problem
Kedge	secondary anchor (lighter)
Keel	fore and aft centre backbone of a ship
Kick	sideways movement produced by prop walk
Lay	direction of twists in strands of rope
Leeward	side away from the wind
Leeway	sideways movement (drift) due to wind / tide
Master	ship owner / person responsible
Make fast / off	secure a rope
Midship	halfway between bow and stern, centre line of vessel
Moor	secure the vessel alongside
Navigation, The	usable part of waterway
Painter	rope from bow of dinghy for towing
Plane (ing)	skid over water surface without ploughing in
Port side	left hand side of vessel looking forward
Prop walk	paddle wheel effect of propeller
Quadrant	curved device on rudder post to improve steering leverage
Quarter	area of ship between side (beam) and stern, corner
Samson post	strong post on deck for towing / securing
Sea anchor	canvas drogue trailed behind vessel to slow it down
Searoom	space to manoeuvre successfully
Ship	large sea-going vessel

_103_

Schipper	Dutch skipper or bargeman
Schipper's Bitter	ideal Dutch liquor for foggy nights
Sill	concrete slab across lock at foot of gates
Skeg	connecting bottom of rudder post to hull or keel
Skipper	person in charge of vessel
Snub	prevent (stop) rope from running out round bitts, cleats etc
Spring	line running fore or aft to another place (dock or vessel)
Standing part	fixed part of a rope which doesn't run (made off at each end)
Starboard	right hand side of vessel looking forward
Steady	maintain a steady course
Steerage way	enough speed to make the rudder effective
Stem	forepost of ship
Stern	back of ship
Surge	controlled movement of rope round bollard / bitts / winch drum
Take a turn	wrap rope round bollard / bitts
Transom	flat or curved stern of a vessel
Under way	ship moving; not anchored, tied up or aground
Upstream	direction current is coming from (towards source)
Vessel	ship or craft of any kind
Wake	water action following a ship
Warps	rope for mooring, moving or anchoring
Warping	doing the above
Wash	waves formed by vessel as it moves forward
Weigh	raise the anchor clear of the ground
Wrap-up	rope or rubbish round propeller

These pages are provided for your own
Notes, Observations and Comments.
They can be removed and sent to the author if you wish.